TALK WIT

IDEAS FOR TEACHERS

TALK WITH ME

Language development through poems, stories, and plays

by Lorelei Liddelow

PEGUIS PUBLISHERS

520 Hargrave Street, Winnipeg, Manitoba, Canada R3A 0X8

First published 1984
by Longman and Cheshire Ltd.,
Melbourne, Australia.

Illustrated by Cindy Hunnum

Canadian Cataloguing in Publication Data

Liddelow, Lorelei
    Talk with me

    (Ideas for teachers)
    ISBN 0-920541-97-6

    1. Language arts (Primary). 2. Language arts (Preschool).
    3. Creative activities and seat work. I. Hunnum, Cindy. II. Title. III. Series.
    LB1528.L533 1990   372.6'044   C90-97042-1

The plays on pages 33, 35, 38, 40, 46, 48, 52, 92 are intended for reproduction in quantities sufficient for classroom use. Permission is hereby granted to reproduce these in suitable quantities for such use.

Acknowledgment
The publishers would like to thank the principal, staff, and children of Chancellor School (Winnipeg) for their cooperation in the preparation of the cover of this book.

Printed and bound in Canada.

Contents

Part Three – Poems and Stories for Classroom Themes

About this book

These poems, stories, and plays are designed to help teachers stimulate the development of children's oral language. The subject matter is closely related to the experience of children. The topics provide the opportunity for all children in the class to participate. Poems and stories in this section can also be used for topics and themes in parts two and three.

Part one includes poems and stories, each with a specific idea for the teacher to develop language activities—conversations, explanations, telephoning, role-playing, and so on.

Part two is a language diary of poems, stories, and plays for special days in the calendar—Halloween, Christmas, Valentine's Day, and so on. The plays may be photocopied for classroom use.

Part three provides further themes for language development: ourselves (at school, at home, in the neighborhood, our senses, our feelings), seasons, animals, holidays, newspapers.

Part One

Poems and Stories
for Language Development

No Cats

Mandy Jones
Lived in an apartment
A high-rise home
A lonely home
Mandy Jones
Wanted a cat
A little cat
To share their home
But the owner said,
"No cats!"

Mandy's mother
Lived there too
In the high-rise home
The lonely home
She bought a mat
For Mandy's cat
So Mandy's cat
Could sit and chat
But the owner said,
"No cats!"

Mandy's mother
Wasn't home
After school
So she was alone
In the high-rise home
The lonely home
Where she wasn't allowed
To have a cat
'Cause the owner said,
"No cats!"

Mandy's mother
Went to work
She worked in a factory
Making shirts
Thinking of Mandy
After school
With only TV
For company
But the owner said,
"No cats!"

A friend of her mother's
Gave Mandy a cat
A furry cat
A purry cat
Who sat on the mat
And liked to chat
And the high-rise home
Was a happy home
Until the owner heard the cat
And the owner said,
"No cats!"

Mandy Jones
Said goodbye to her cat
And gave him back
And washed his mat
And put it away
In the high-rise home
The lonely home
And that was that
And the owner said,
"No cats!"

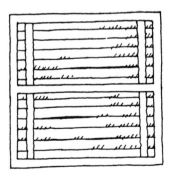

Conversations

A selected topic, such as this poem, may be used to stimulate general conversation among children, and as a beginning activity for the language program. Through imaginative questioning the teacher should extend the subject matter and relate it to the children's experiences. Appreciative listening and courteous participation should be encouraged. "Show and tell" activities and dramatized conversations that involve role playing may also be used to develop fluency and confidence.

1. Teacher reads the poem and guides the conversation.
   - Children talk about the meaning of the poem:
        the story
        characters
        life in a high-rise apartment building

   - Children talk about the poem's mood:
        Mandy's feelings
        her mother's
        the owner's
        the cat's
        their feelings about the poem

2. Teacher guides the conversation towards the wider experience of the children.
   - Children talk about animals' feelings:
        in backyards
        zoos
        farms
        circuses
        national parks
        the natural environment
   - Children talk about their own experiences with animals:
        pets
        strays
        S.P.C.A.
        visits to the vet

3. Teacher re-reads the poem or selections from it and asks the children to think about Mandy as they listen.

A Sarah Salad

Mrs. Withnell was taking her class for a picnic in the park. Everyone remembered to bring lunch except Sarah. "Never mind, Sarah," said Mrs. Withnell. "We'll make you a lunch. It's lucky I went shopping before school this morning."

So Mrs. Withnell helped Sarah to:

1. Spread out some clean paper
2. Grate a carrot (for a dress)
3. Grate some cheese (for hair)
4. Cut a boiled egg in half (for a face)
5. Cut a piece of celery into two short pieces and two long pieces (for arms and legs)
6. Choose two currants (for eyes)
7. Choose one raisin (for a nose)
8. Choose an orange slice (for a mouth)
9. Spread a lettuce leaf on a plate and put the salad together to make a Sarah Salad.

So Sarah took her Sarah Salad and off she went with Mrs. Withnell and her class to the park.

Explanations

"Do and Tell" language activities develop the children's ability to describe a sequence of actions clearly and concisely. It is important that the children participate in the preparation of the salad.

1. Teacher tells the story.

2. Children discuss the recipe: the ingredients and the sequence of actions. Nine cards outlining the directions could be made. Children could then sort them in the correct order to prepare the salad.

3. Children make their salads.

4. Children help the teacher to record the recipe in the Class Recipe Book.

Our Family Tree

A family is like a tree.
We are its branches, roots, and leaves.
We belong to our family tree.

Grandma and Grandpa begin, you see.
Their place is at the top of the tree.
They belong to our family tree.

Then Mother and Father, Baby and Me.
We come next on the family tree.
We belong to our family tree.

Then uncles and aunts appear on the tree
And cousins Jane and Timothy.
They belong to our family tree.

Tootles our cat, and our dog Snoopy,
And Pepper and Salt, our two budgies.
They belong to our family tree.

People, children, pets, babies,
Each has his place upon the tree.
They all belong to our family tree.

Picture Talks

Talking about pictures develops the children's oral vocabulary. Apart from pictures provided by the teacher, children should talk about pictures they have created themselves or discovered in books, magazines, newspapers, and family photograph albums.

1. Children are seated where they will be able to see the teacher and the picture.

2. Teacher reads the poem and encourages the children to join in speaking the refrain.

3. Teacher displays a family-tree mobile of the family (made from coat hangers and magazine pictures).

4. Children are given ample time to look at the pictures.

5. Children discuss the pictures. Teacher encourages careful observation and individual interpretation through
   - questions related to the pictures of the family
   - questions related to the children's experiences (who are the people on *your* family tree? names, ages, appearances, relatives, friends, neighbors, pets, leisure, occupations)
   - questions which extend the subject matter (famous families, animal families, storyland families)
   NOTE: It is important to accept everyone children think of as part of the family.

6. Complete-sentence answers and imaginative use of vocabulary are encouraged and entered in the Class Dictionary.

7. If the children wish, the poem may be reread, this time with the children's participation.

The Pound

We've lost our little puppy.
He's spotted white and brown.
He has a tail that wags all day.
His ears go up and down.

Our puppy's name is Clifford
As in the reading book.
Oh dear, oh dear, where can he be?
We've looked, and looked and looked.

When Dad came home he said to us,
"I know where he'll be found.
Find the number in the 'phone book
And ring the local pound."

We found the telephone number.
We wrote the number down.
We lifted the receiver.
We heard the dial-tone sound.

We dialled the number carefully
And got through to the pound.
"Our puppy's lost," we told them,
"Do you know if he's been found?"

We told them what he looks like—
Spotted white and brown—
About his tail that wags all day
And his ears going up and down.

"Don't worry," said the nice kind man,
"Your puppy's in the pound.
We found him crying in the park
But now he's safe and sound."

So off we went with father
To fetch our Clifford home.
We must take better care of him.
We mustn't let him roam.

And here's our little puppy
Spotted white and brown.
He's so glad to see us
And we're so glad he's found.

Telephoning

Role playing of telephone conversations helps children to refine social language skills.

1. Teacher reads the poem and the children discuss their experiences related to the subject matter.

2. Teacher helps the children learn telephone techniques, for example
   - Finding the number of the local pound in the directory
   - Miming the lifting of the receiver
   - Listening for the dial tone (a tape-recording could be used)
   - Dialing the number
   - Giving greeting and own name when someone answers, then beginning the conversation (discuss the content with children)
   - Speaking clearly and courteously
   - Concluding politely, replacing the receiver

3. Children role-play in pairs as owner of lost puppy and pound-keeper.

4. A fluent pair repeat their conversation before the class, using toy telephones.

Classroom Manners

Miss Moon's class
Says "Please" and "Thank you."
Miss Moon's class
Says "May I" too,
And they say, "I beg your pardon,"
As all well-mannered children do.

Miss Moon's class
Say their "Good Mornings"
In a nice, bright, cheerful way,
And they use their nice bright voices
When they read
To her each day.

Miss Moon's class
Learns how to take turns,
That's the right way to behave,
And they keep their desks so neatly,
And they put each book
Away.

Miss Moon's class
Can tuck their chairs in.
They don't fuss
Or bang or crash,
And they know to walk out quietly
For a story on the mat.

Miss Moon's class
Are sensible people.
They keep all
Their classroom rules.
It's so easy to be courteous
And enjoy one's days at school.

Courtesy

Young children should learn appropriate social behavior. Role playing of familiar situations will help children develop acceptable standards.

1. Teacher reads the poem and develops the subject matter to include manners at home, in stores, on the bus.

2. Children role play social situations, for example, good manners at the table:
   • each child makes his own table setting from recycled materials
   • groups of four role play good manners at the table

Classroom Helpers

Pencils,
And stamps,
And scissors,
And paper.

Pictures,
And books,
And pads
For our notes.

Ropes,
And hoops,
And balls,
And beanbags.

Jigsaws,
And blocks,
AND MORE TO
COME!

Shells,
And crabs,
And worms,
And tadpoles.

Bells,
And cymbals,
And horns,
And drums.

Puppets,
And masks,
And lipsticks,
And dress-ups.

Telephones,
Fish tanks,
WE FORGOT
SOME!

Clay,
And glue,
And paints,
And tissues.

Flowers,
And plants,
And seeds,
And nuts.

Cassettes,
And records,
And mikes,
And earphones.

Who
Will look
After them?
EVERYONE!

Group Discussions

Young children feel less inhibited when speaking in small groups. They learn acceptable group behavior by taking turns to speak and by listening politely to others.

1. Teacher reads the poem as motivation and suggests to the children they might like to work in small groups to plan a class duty roster.

2. Teacher explains to the children how to work in small groups.
   - Children discuss the group-leaders' duties:
     Announce the discussion topic.
     Ask each child in turn to give his or her opinion.
     Make sure the other children in the group listen.
     Stand and give the group's report.
   - Children discuss a group member's duties:
     Wait quietly for his turn to speak.
     Speak clearly.
     Listen politely.
     Help to form a group opinion, or decision.

3. Teacher announces the topic, "Planning Our Class Duty Roster." The class is encouraged to discuss the topic briefly to stimulate the children's ideas:
   WHAT jobs have to be done?
   WHEN?
   HOW?
   WHY?
   WHO will do them?

4. Teacher may provide a brief summary on the blackboard (to assist the children).

5. Teacher allocates the leaders and groups and places.
   - One group at a time moves into place.
   - Groups discuss the topic.
   - Teacher supervises and concludes the discussion when appropriate.
   - Leaders give their reports.
   - Children may ask questions.

6. Teacher comments constructively on the reports and thanks the leaders for their efforts.

The New Boy

A new boy stood at the principal's door,
He'd never been to that school before.
He was a French boy, his name was Jean Paul.
He was eight-years-old and very small.

His mother kissed him "goodbye" and left,
And Jean Paul stood there, by himself.
The Principal said, "Come with me,
I'll take you down to your class, grade three."

A lady met them, she seemed quite kind,
"Bonjour, Jean Paul," she said with a smile.
She had a soft voice and her face was nice.
"I'm Miss Armstrong," she said. "Do come inside."

She sat Jean Paul down at a table for four,
"This is Choong," she said, "from Singapore,
And this is Hans, and this is Sue,
And this is Henri, he's French too."

"Now, Jean Paul, if you feel confused
Just ask Henri, he'll help you.
At recess we'll take you on a tour
And show you all around the school."

Miss Armstrong gave him a map which showed
All the school places he'd have to know.
Then she and Jean Paul walked around with Henri
'Til there wasn't a place Jean Paul hadn't seen.

The classrooms, the bathrooms, the playground too.
The library, the bike racks, and nurse's room.
He knew where to go, he knew what to do,
And Jean Paul stopped feeling new.

Giving Directions

Learning to use exact words to give directions to familiar places helps children to use language accurately and concisely.

1. Teacher reads the poem and discusses it with the children.

2. Teacher pins a large plan of the school on the bulletin board.

3. Children discuss its features and using exact words for places, distances, turns, they explain how to get from their classroom to other school areas.

4. A school walk involving measurement would help to make this a real experience.

5. Make a map of the district. Children explain how to get to their home, to the store, and so on.

What is Thunder?

Thunder is rolling around the sky.
Have you ever wondered why?

Thunder comes and thunder goes.
How does thunder come and go?

Thunder and lightning are so frightening.
Why does thunder follow lightning?

What makes thunder sound so loud
Way up there among the clouds?

There are answers to this wonder.
Try and find out "What is thunder?"

News Sessions

To avoid the boring daily ritual of this activity, conduct a news session only when something significant and of common interest has occurred, for example, "The First Storm."

1. If the children have experienced a storm the previous night, or that day, teacher could select the above poem to read.

2. Teacher holds a brief discussion to stimulate ideas:
   - Where were you when the storm started?
   - What did you see? hear?
   - What came first, the lightning or the thunder? Why?
   - What happened at your house? (leaking roof? frightened pets? trees blown down?)
   - Go to the library to see if there are any books that can answer these questions.

3. Children move into groups to tell news.

4. One child from each group could be selected to tell his/or her version to the class if he wishes.

5. To vary presentation children could use a mock microphone or TV set, or puppets.

6. Teacher comments positively on content, vocabulary, voice usage, ability to answer questions.

Easter Bunny

The children at St. Dominic's School often brought their toys and books to school.

One day Louisa brought her Easter Bunny.

Miss Lucas decided that the children should get to know Easter Bunny better.

That afternoon she played them a tape recording of Easter Bunny being interviewed at the airport.

(Miss Lucas had made the recording at lunch time. She had disguised her voice to make it sound like an interviewer's.)

"Good morning, listeners, this is your roving reporter at the airport. There is great excitement here. We are awaiting the arrival of a world-famous celebrity. His plane has just landed, and it is taxiing up the tarmac. The door is opening and here he is—Easter Bunny. He is being ushered into the V.I.P. lounge where we will interview him."

Miss Lucas stopped the tape recorder.

"Listen carefully to the first question," she said, and she turned the tape recorder on.

"Good morning, Easter Bunny. Welcome to our city. We know you have brought your family with you. How many children do you have, and what are their names?"

Then Miss Lucas said, "We are not going to hear Easter Bunny's answer," and she turned off the tape recorder.

She explained that the children had to pretend to be Easter Bunny and imagine what his answer might be.

The children thought carefully.

"I think Easter Bunny would have two children," said Andrew, "and I think their names would be Brer and Peter."

Other children had different ideas.

Melissa used an Easter Bunny voice when she gave her answer.

She sounded just like Easter Bunny.

Then Miss Lucas played the rest of the questions one by one, and the children made up Easter Bunny answers.

Here are the questions:

"You have made friends with thousands of children, Easter Bunny. What memories do you have of your own childhood?"

"We have heard you tried many jobs before you became famous. Could you tell us about some of them?"

"We know that famous people are busy people, but we'd like to know what you do in your free time, Easter Bunny?"

"You have said you don't intend to be an Easter Bunny forever. What are your plans for the future?"

"What is your advice to young people who would like to be as famous as Easter Bunny?"

The children made up some very clever Easter Bunny answers.

Then Miss Lucas played the end of the tape recording.

The interviewer said, "Thank you, Easter Bunny, for allowing us to interview you. We hope you enjoy your visit to our city. This is your roving reporter saying 'Goodbye' from the airport."

The children had enjoyed being Easter Bunny. Everyone was glad Louisa had brought him to school.

Asking and Answering Questions

Young children should be encouraged to ask questions at every opportunity, for example, after a news session, a radio broadcast, a television program. They should learn to give sentence answers, not one-word responses to questions, for example, "Answer me in a story, Fiona." Teachers need to refine their questioning techniques to ensure answers which give information, ideas, opinions.

1. Teacher reads the story.

2. Children make up their own Easter Bunny questions and answers.

3. Children work in pairs as Easter Bunny and his interviewer, and role play their interviews.

A Weather Riddle

I'm a forecast on your radio,
I'm a map on your TV,
I'm a chart on your classroom wall—
Do you know me?

I worry every farmer,
And the sailors on the sea,
But I help to make your garden grow—
Do you know me?

I try to make myself keep fine
To please the family.
Especially at holiday time—
Do you know me?

My name begins with a *W,*
I also have two *E*s.
Add *A* and *T* and *H* and *R*—
Now you know me!

Reporting

Children should be able to describe a sequence of events or ideas accurately, and to express their opinions confidently.

1. Teacher reads the riddle and children guess.

2. Teacher introduces a Class Weather Chart, children discuss its aspects and complete the details of that day's weather:
   DATE, SEASON, TEMPERATURE, CLOUD, RAINFALL, WIND

3. Children move into groups of six and practice their weather reports.

4. Each child reports on one aspect.

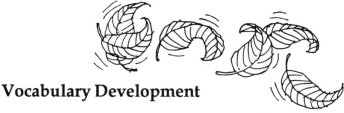

Vocabulary Development

Children's instinctive love of words should be enriched.

1. Teacher reads the poem. Children discuss their meal-time tastes.

2. Teacher provides food samples, for example:

• TOUCH AND TELL: (Put in box, where children can feel but not see.)	dish of jello eggshells dough a wishbone
• SMELL AND TELL	cheese mashed egg banana sardines
• TASTE AND TELL:	sweet sour salty bitter samples

3. Children experiment, identify, and describe tastes.

4. Build up a "Tastes Book" featuring the children's vocabulary (gibberish, single words, phrases, sentences, stories).

Play Lunch

Crunch, Crunch!
Munch, Munch!
An apple for
My play lunch.
Bite, chew,
Bite, chew,
Crisp and sweet
And juicy too.
Crunch, Crunch!
Munch, Munch!
I wonder what
I'll have for lunch.

The Sad Story of Baby Bear

The Three Bears went
For a walk in the woods
To wait for their porridge
To cool.
They found a nice
Big shady tree
Beside a quiet pool.

Father Bear read
His newspaper,
And Mother Bear
Started to knit,
And Baby Bear
Threw stones in the pool,
And paddled around
For a bit.

Father Bear
Fell fast asleep,
And Mother Bear
Started to doze,
And naughty little
Baby Bear
He ran off
On tippy-toes.

He wandered deep
Into the woods.
He walked into
Storyland.
He met Henny Penny
And Three Little Pigs,
Snow White and the
Gingerbread Man.

Red Riding Hood
Went trotting by,
And Mr. Wolf,
Slinketty sly,
Hansel and Gretel,
The witch in her house,
Three Billy Goats Gruff,
And the Lion and the Mouse.

Cinderella came along,
And the Seven Dwarfs
Singing a song.
Rapunzel with her
Long, gold hair,
The Frog Prince and
Aladdin were there.

Suddenly,
They all went home,
And Baby Bear
Was left alone.
"I'll go home too,"
Thought Baby Bear,
"I wish I knew
How to get there."

Do you know
The story's end?
Did he get help
From his friends?
Did Father Bear,
And Mother Bear too,
Come looking for him?
I don't know, do you?

Perhaps the folk
From Storyland
Will come for him
And take his hand,
And show Baby Bear
The way to go,
Or, better still,
Will take him home.

Thinking caps on,
Work out a way
To help Baby Bear
Find his home today.
Remember this,
Each one of you,
Don't wander away,
Or you'll get lost too.

Storymaking

Children learn to improvise a proper sequence of events when making up stories to tell.

1. Teacher reads the poem.

2. Through questioning the teacher guides the children to create a story plot, for example:

• THE BEGINNING:	Where was Baby Bear? Who else was there? What sort of place was it? Why was he there? How did he feel? So what did he do?
• MIDDLE:	Who came along? What were their names? What did they say? What happened next?
• ENDING:	What happened to them all? How did the story end? How did Baby Bear feel then?

3. Teacher may need to retell the story, weaving the children's ideas into a storyline. Most young children, however, could retell the story without prompting.

4. After several "whole-class" stories have been made up, small-group storymaking could be introduced.

5. Stories could be recorded for use in the Listening Corner.

Storyland Rhymes

One, two,
A spell on you.

Three, four,
Wolf at the door.

Five, six,
Witch's tricks.

Seven, eight,
Giant's awake!

Nine, ten,
Little Red Hen.

That was fun,
Let's do it again.

A, B, C, D,
Owl and Pussy went to sea.

E, F, G, H,
Goldilocks ran through the gate.

I, J, K, L,
Someone had a lamp to sell.

M, N, O, P,
Rumpelstiltskin came to tea.

Q, R, S, T,
Who fell down the pig's chimney?

U, V, W, X,
Cinderella had a dirty dress.

Last of all, Y and Z,
Now you know the alphabet.

Descriptions

Guessing games develop careful observation and stimulate descriptive language.

1. Teacher reads the rhymes, and describes one of the characters, for example:
   I am a little girl.
   I have gold hair.
   I go into people's places without being invited.
   Who am I?

2. Children guess.

3. Teacher encourages a wider use of vocabulary, for example:

   I am a curious little girl.
   I have golden locks.
   I trespass on other people's property.
   Who am I?

4. Teacher suggests "guide words," for example, size, shape, coloring, personality, voice, gait.

5. Children move into groups of four, and the teacher gives each group a familiar storyland character to describe. You may want to give younger children a guide to follow, for example,
   I am _____
   I have _____
   I (something they do) _____
   Who am I?

6. Class guesses.

Abigail Solves Them All

OAKVILLE: Abigail Jones, aged seven, has solved a string of mysterious thefts.

Last week Abigail, from Main Street, Kingston, went into a shop at Kingston Mall leaving her backpack and her favorite toy bear at the door.

When she came out she saw a black Labrador dog dashing off with the bear in its mouth, so Abigail set off in pursuit, but the dog disappeared.

On Friday afternoon she saw the Labrador on the prowl again.

She followed it to its home and saw it jump on a bed in the back room of a house.

In the room was her bear, surrounded by a collection of missing footwear.

Abigail Jones is a detective.
You know what a detective is, don't you?
A detective is someone whose job is to solve mysteries, and catch thieves and burglars and people like that.
The amazing thing about Abigail is that although she is a detective, she is only seven-years-old.
It happened like this.
Abigail lives on Main Street, Kingston.
One Monday afternoon, on her way home from school, Abigail went into a shop to buy an ice cream cone.
She put her backpack and her teddy bear near the door of the shop. (Abigail often took her teddy bear to school.)
When she came out of the shop she saw a big, black Labrador dog, with her teddy bear in its mouth, running away down the street.
Abigail ran after that naughty dog as fast as she could, but she could not catch it.

When she came to the corner of the street the dog was nowhere to be seen.
Abigail was very unhappy. Where was her darling teddy bear?
Where could that big black dog have taken him?
Abigail started to think very carefully.
She made a plan.
Every afternoon, after school, she watched for that black Labrador dog.

Nothing happened on Tuesday afternoon, or Wednesday, or Thursday.
Then on Friday afternoon, Abigail saw the Labrador on the prowl again.
She hurried after it as quickly as she could.
She followed it down the street and around the corner.
She saw it trot through the gate of a house, down the garden path, and around to the back.
Abigail ran after the dog.

Through the gate she went, and down the path and around to the back of the house.
No one was about.
Abigail stood on tiptoe and looked through a window into the back room of the house.
There on a bed was the big, black, Labrador dog, and in one corner of the room, amongst a pile of children's thongs and shoes and balls sat... Abigail's teddy bear.

How happy Abigail was.
There was her teddy bear safe and sound.
That naughty dog was a thief.
All those shoes and things belonged to other children just like Abigail.
Abigail ran home as fast as she could and told her mother the whole story.
That evening Abigail and her parents went around to the Labrador's home and saw the lady who lived there.
The lady went straight into the back room and fetched Abigail's teddy bear and gave him to Abigail.
Abigail hugged him very tightly and kissed his nose.
Then the grown-ups had a long talk.
Abigail did not know what they were talking about.
She didn't bother to listen.
Abigail was too busy talking to her teddy bear.

Retelling Stories

Newspaper articles, headlines, photographs, and captions can be used as a basis for retelling stories.

1. Teacher reads the article.

2. Through questioning the teacher guides the children to express the content of the newspaper article in story form:
   • developing a situation
   • adding characters
   • producing dialogue and action

3. Children retell their improvised stories in small-group and partner-work situations.

The Hospital Kit

We had nothing to do
On a wet afternoon
Then Grandma arrived
For an hour or two.

We took her coat
And her feathery hat
And she sat down with Mother
To have a chat.

She gave us a box
And said with a smile,
"I think you'll enjoy
What you find inside."

We untied the string
And opened it—
A Doctors' and Nurses'
Hospital Kit!

We gave dear Grandma
A hug and a kiss.
We're going to have
Such fun with this!

Nurses' caps,
A doctor's white coat,
And a little flashlight
To look down sore throats.

A stethoscope,
A thermometer too,
Tweezers, bandages,
Bottles, and tubes.

We'll turn our bedroom
Into a ward,
And put "HOSPITAL"
On the bedroom door.

At last our patients
Are tucked up tight,
And everything's tidy
And clean and bright.

You be the doctor
And start your rounds.
I'll follow you—
I'll be Nurse Brown.

I've taken each pulse
And each temperature too.
They've all had their medicine
Ready for you.

Thank you, nurse.
I'll start right away.
I have lots of patients
To see today.

Hello, Raggedy Ann
How are you?
You've really caught
A bad dose of 'flu.

And Bride Doll,
How's your throat today?
Feeling less painful
Than yesterday?

Good Morning, Teddy,
Your tummy still aches?
Oh dear, I'm afraid
We must operate.

"May I come in?"
Grandma said at the door,
"I've come to see
Your hospital ward."

"You have worked hard,"
She said with a smile,
"May I stay
For a little while?"

We thanked her again
For her lovely gift.
We're having such fun
With our Hospital Kit.

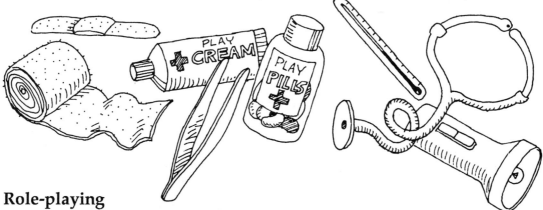

Role-playing

Young children enjoy dressing up and dramatic play. They live their roles, exploring language as they improvise words, dialogue, action.

1. Teacher reads the poem.

2. Children discuss "hospital experiences" and names of people who work in hospitals.

3. Using simple costumes and properties made from recycled materials (nurses' caps, stethoscopes, bandages, thermometers), children role-play hospital situations.

A Mother's Day

Tick Tock,
Tick tock,
"Time to get up,"
Says the clock.

Breakfast's ready,
Lunches packed.
Into the car
We're quickly stacked.

Mother drives carefully
Obeying each rule,
A kiss and a hug
And then into school.

Tick tock,
Tick tock,
"Time for housework,"
Says the clock.

Home again
With chores to do—
Sweeping, cooking,
Sewing too.

A phone call to Grandma,
A quick cup of tea,
Shopping to do,
It's a quarter to three!

Tick tock,
Tick tock,
"Pick up the children,"
Says the clock.

Children chatter
In her ear
All the day's doings
For her to hear.

"Don't forget, Mummy,
It's brownies today!"
"Where are my boots, Mom,
I need them to play!"

Tick tock,
Tick tock,
"Time to get dinner,"
Says the clock.

When the dishes
Are cleared away
She checks the homework
For today.

Children are bathed
And put to bed.
They ask to have
A story read.

Tick tock,
Tick tock,
"Time to yourself,"
Says the clock.

Mother at last
Is all alone.
At last she has
Some time of her own.

She'll spend it with Daddy
Staying home—
Just Mommy and Daddy
On their own.

Tick tock,
Tick tock,
Says the clock,
Tick tock,
Tick tock, Tick tock.

Listening

Communication is a two-way experience. Children should learn to be appreciative, critical listeners as well as articulate speakers.

1. Teacher reads "A Mother's Day."

2. Teacher plays a tape recording of the sounds of a mother's day clock ticking, alarm, whistling kettle, vacuum cleaner, washing machine, end of child's bedtime story, TV news. Teacher can ask some of the children to tape their own sounds.

3. Children identify the sounds and recall sequence.

A Beanstalk Rhyme

Up and up
And up I go.
Goodbye Mother,
Down below.

The beanstalk sways
And twists and winds.
I'm leaving home
Far behind!

Up and up
And up I climb.
At the top
What shall I find?

At last I'm there.
What's that I see?
A giant's house
But I haven't a key.

The door's ajar.
I'll creep inside.
If someone comes
I'll have to hide.

I'll look around.
I've grown quite bold.
What's over there?
Some bags of gold!

Suddenly
A dreadful roar.
I've never heard
That sound before.

Fee, fie,
Fo, fum!
Where can I run?
The Giant's come!

Messages

The role-playing of messages helps to develop careful listening and thinking and clear speaking.

1. Teacher reads the poem.

2. Children discuss the story of "Jack and the Beanstalk."

3. Teacher role-plays Jack's mother giving Jack a message, for example:

    "Jack, fetch the cow, sell it at the market, and use the money to buy food."

4. Teacher repeats the message, pausing at the ends of phrases, for example:

    WHO: Jack
    WHAT: fetch the cow and sell it
    WHERE: at the market
    WHY: and use the money to buy food.

5. Children role-play the message in pairs. For example, mother gives the message to Jack who repeats it to mother.

6. Children invent their own storyland messages, for example:

    Mother Bear to Baby Bear
    Mother to Red Riding Hood
    Master to Puss-in-Boots

Our Music Teacher

Mr. Wood can play the piano
Mr. Wood can play the flute
Mr. Wood can play the trumpet
Mr. Wood writes music too.

Mr. Wood's our music teacher
He teaches music to each class
We learn singing and recorder
And we love to play the brass.

Mr. Wood teaches us on Fridays
What will be today's new song?
We are learning to read music
It sounds awful when we're wrong!

Mr. Woods plays music for us
"Was the music loud or soft?
Sad or happy?" he will ask us.
"Did you want to dance or not?"

Mr. Wood takes us to concerts
He takes us to the ballet too
Nutcracker's our favorite ballet
Popcorn is our favorite tune.

Mr. Wood's our music teacher
He is kind to everyone
We can't wait until next Friday
Making music's so much fun!

Announcements

Language experiences of a more formal nature should be included in the repertoire of children's communicative skills; for example, the speaking requirements situation of a school assembly.

1. Teacher reads the poem.

2. Teacher and children discuss class excursions (concerts, ballet, art galleries, museums).

3. Children prepare an announcement to be made at the school assembly. Teacher lists guide words on the chalkboard:

    WHO: Mr. Wood's class
    WHAT: is going to the ballet
    WHERE: at the Concert Hall
    WHEN: on Tuesday, the fifth of December.
    (HOW and WHY may be included)

4. In groups of four, children practice the announcement. Each child announces a specific aspect. Children could use mock microphones (match boxes on popsicle sticks) to improve voice projection.

5. A fluent group could present the announcement at the school assembly or over the public address system.

Say "Good Morning" to a Tree

Say "Good Morning" to a tree,
Ask about his family,
His branches, roots, flowers, leaves,
Say "Good Morning" to a tree.

Say "Good Morning" to a tree,
Chat about his community.
Of ants and grubs, birds and bees,
Say "Good Morning" to a tree.

Say "Good Morning" to a tree,
Say "Thank you for your company,
And all the gifts you give to me,"
Say "Good Morning" to a tree.

Choral Speaking

Young children delight in rhythm and rhyme. They should experiment with individual and group recitation of poetry.

1. Teacher takes children outside. They select a tree, sit beneath it, and the teacher reads the poem.

2. Children discuss the poem's "story"—its meaning, the feelings it evokes, and the children's experiences related to the subject matter.

3. The teacher and the children prepare the orchestration of the poem (three speaking groups, one for each verse; class speaks the refrain).

4. Teacher patterns the speaking of the poem.

5. Children recite the poem to the tree, say goodbye to the tree, and return to the classroom.

Part Two

Poems, Stories, and Plays
for Special Days

SEPTEMBER: *Beginning School*

Emily's First Day of School

Emily, Emily
Open your eyes.
Emily, come on
It's time to rise.

Emily, Emily
Don't you remember?
Emily, school has started,
It's September.

Emily, Emily
What is today?
Emily knows
It's School's First Day.

Emily, Emily
Let's get dressed.
Emily, try to
Look your best.

Emily, Emily
Don't stand and chat.
Emily, let's get
Your backpack packed.

Emily, Emily
Kiss me "Goodbye."
Emily, have a
Lovely time.

Emily, Emily
I miss you.
Emily, do you
Miss me too?

Emily, Emily
Wrote a poem.
Emily sang it
Skipping home.

Emily, Emily
Home at last!
Emily, the first
Day is past.

Emily, Emily
What's that you say?
Emily, you've had
A lovely day.

Emily, Emily
Come upstairs.
Emily, don't forget
Your prayers.

Emily, Emily
Turn out the light.
Emily, time
To say "Goodnight."

OCTOBER: *Halloween*

A Halloween Riddle

HALLOWEEN

What does it mean?
Is it a color
Like red or green?

HALLOWEEN

What word is that?
Is it a cat or a bat
Or a hat?

HALLOWEEN

What does it say?
Hello? Goodbye?
Have a nice day?

HALLOWEEN

What a mystery!
I'll have to look
In my dictionary.

Pumpkin

Who's inside
That pumpkin mask?
Who can it be?
We're too frightened to ask.

Is it a ghost
In that pumpkin head?
Or a skeleton
From its graveyard bed?

Perhaps it's a witch
With a pumpkin face.
It could be a goblin
From outer space.

It's watching us
With its horrible stare.
Whoever it is
I wish it weren't there.

It's Halloween

A special night
Comes once a year
Thirty-first of October
It's almost here.

On that night
You must take care
Strange things happen
So beware.

Ghosts and goblins
Are waiting for you
As shadows flit
Across the moon.

Jack-o'-lanterns
Come out that night
They have terrible teeth
So keep out of sight.

Witches wail
Bats scream
Ghosts moan
It's Halloween.

Wizard Mellow

1 Once long ago
Lived a king and a queen
In the wonderful Land
Of Make-Believe.

2 The king was kind
And strong and just.
His people loved him
Very much.

3 The queen, his wife
Was wise and sweet
With long golden hair
Down to her feet.

4 But she often cried
When she was alone
For she and the king
Had no child of their own.

5 At last the king spoke
To his wizard, Mellow,
Who was a remarkably
Clever fellow.

6 "Read your books
Look up your files
Work your magic
And make the queen smile."

7 Wizard Mellow
Began at once.
He didn't bother
To stop for lunch.

8 He said, "Bring clowns
And some acrobats too.
They might make the queen smile.
Let's hope they do."

9 The clowns did their tricks
Ever so neatly
But the queen didn't smile,
She just thanked them sweetly.

10 "I'll plan a surprise,"
Thought Wizard Mellow
And he caught a sunbeam
All golden and yellow.

11 He put it on
The queen's breakfast tray
But "How kind of you,"
Was all she could say.

12 So Wizard Mellow
Went far and wide
And up and down
The countryside.

13 One night he came
To a little town.
He heard a cry
And when he looked down...

14 There on the doorstep
All alone
Were two little babies
On their own.

15 "They're orphans
Only one week old.
Nobody wants them,"
He was told.

16 "I'll take them myself,"
Said dear old Mellow.
I told you he was
A remarkable fellow.

17 He called the baby boy Jim,
And the baby girl Sue.
He gave them their bottles
And cuddled them too.

18 He returned to the palace
And said to the queen,
"I've two presents for you
You are sure to enjoy."

19 The queen clapped her hands
And then she smiled
And then she laughed
And then the queen cried.

20 She kissed baby boy Jim,
And baby girl Sue.
And she gave Wizard Mellow
A little kiss too.

21 So the queen is a mother
And the king is a father
And old Wizard Mellow's
A proud godfather.

22 And happy live
The king and queen
In the wonderful Land
Of Make-Believe.

OCTOBER: *Halloween*

Three Witches

1 Three witches flew
Into town today
Parked their broomsticks
And said, "Let's stay."
  Ha, Ha, Ho, Ho,
  Hee, Hee, Hee, Hee.
They went to the beach.
They went shopping too.
They went to the park,
They went to the zoo.
  Ha, Ha, Ho, Ho,
  Hee, Hee, Hee, Hee.

2 They went to golf
'Til half-past two
Then roller-skated
All afternoon.
  Ha, Ha, Ho, Ho,
  Hee, Hee, Hee, Hee.
We got to know them
Rather well.
Each funny old witch
Had a tale to tell.
  Ha, Ha, Ho, Ho,
  Hee, Hee, Hee, Hee.

3 I am a witch.
Haggy-Baggy's my name.
I'm wrinkled and hairy
And toothless and plain.
  Ha, Ha, Ho, Ho,
  Hee, Hee, Hee, Hee.
I'm making this spell
From animal bits.
I know it is cruel
But nothing else fits.
  Ha, Ha, Ho, Ho,
  Hee, Hee, Hee, Hee.

4 Sliced tongue of snake
Chopped tail of rat
Peeled eye of toad
Minced wing of bat
  Ha, Ha, Ho, Ho,
  Hee, Hee, Hee, Hee.
But the spell didn't work,
"That's that," I said.
"No animal bits
I'll use herbs instead."
  Ha, Ha, Ho, Ho,
  Hee, Hee, Hee, Hee.

5 I am a witch.
   Hoity-Toity's my name.
   I'm spiteful and cranky
   And stuck-up and vain.
     Ha, Ha, Ho, Ho,
     Hee, Hee, Hee, Hee.
   I like making spells
   That do people harm.
   This spell of mine
   Will work like a charm.
     Ha, Ha, Ho, Ho,
     Hee, Hee, Hee, Hee.

6 A teaspoon of stardust
   Mixed with champagne
   Makes plain girls ugly
   And pretty girls plain.
     Ha, Ha, Ho, Ho,
     Hee, Hee, Hee, Hee.
   I make everyone cry
   But I'm not really glad
   So I'll stop making spells
   That make people sad.
     Ha, Ha, Ho, Ho,
     Hee, Hee, Hee, Hee.

7 I am a witch.
   Greedy-Gutsy's my name.
   I look like a dustbin.
   I smell like a drain.
     Ha, Ha, Ho, Ho,
     Hee, Hee, Hee, Hee.
   I'm bloated and greasy
   And spotty and fat.
   I'd like to be thin
   Not fat like that.
     Ha, Ha, Ho, Ho,
     Hee, Hee, Hee, Hee.

8 I eat everything
   On the kitchen shelf.
   Perhaps I should put
   A spell on myself!
     Ha, Ha, Ho, Ho,
     Hee, Hee, Hee, Hee.
   I'll go to a Charm School
   And Weight Watchers too.
   I'll make fat people thin,
   That's what I'll do.
     Ha, Ha, Ho, Ho,
     Hee, Hee, Hee, Hee.

9 Three witches flew
   Into town today.
   They had a good time
   Then they flew away.
     Ha, Ha, Ho, Ho,
     Hee, Hee, Hee, Hee.
   They wrote us a letter
   To tell all the town
   They'd changed their lifestyle.
   They're much happier now.
     Ha, Ha, Ho, Ho,
     Hee, Hee, Hee, Hee.

10 They said we were kind.
   They sent us a gift.
   Guess what it was—
   A magic broomstick!
     Ha, Ha, Ho, Ho,
     Hee, Hee, Hee, Hee.
   We all take turns
   To fly around.
   Life's much more fun
   In our town now.
     Ha, Ha, Ho, Ho,
     Hee, Hee, Hee, Hee.

OCTOBER: *Universal Children's Day*

Let's Be Friends

Children enter and form five groups facing audience.

ALL:	Let's be friends. *Groups turn, face back of stage, sit.*
CHILD ONE:	*Stands, face audience.* Kalimera.
GROUP ONE:	Kalimera.
CHILD ONE:	My name is Yiorgo. I come from Greece.
GROUP ONE:	*Stand, form a circle with Yiorgo, march around, saying:* Isn't it fun To meet someone different. Isn't it fun To make new friends. Isn't it fun To say to someone, "My name is... Let's be friends." *Sit, facing audience.*
CHILD TWO:	*Stands, facing audience.* Apa Khabar.
GROUP TWO:	Apa Khabar.
CHILD TWO:	My name is Ali. I come from Malaysia.
GROUP TWO:	*Stand, form a circle with Ali, march around, saying:* Isn't it fun To meet someone different. Isn't it fun To make new friends. Isn't it fun To say to someone "My name is... Let's be friends." *Sit, facing audience.*
CHILD THREE:	*Stands, faces audience.* Ohiyoo.
GROUP THREE:	Ohiyoo.

CHILD THREE:	My name is Mayami. I come from Japan.
GROUP THREE:	*Stand, form a circle with Mayami, march around saying:*

Isn't it fun
To meet someone different.
Isn't it fun
To make new friends.
Isn't it fun
To say to someone
"My name is...
Let's be friends."

Sit, facing audience.

CHILD FOUR:	*Stands, faces audience.*
	Shalom.
GROUP FOUR:	Shalom.
CHILD FOUR:	My name is Esther. I come from Israel.
GROUP FOUR:	*Stand, form a circle with Esther, march around, saying:*

Isn't it fun
To meet someone different.
Isn't it fun
To make new friends.
Isn't it fun
To say to someone
"My name is...
Let's be friends."

Sit, facing audience.

CHILD FIVE:	*Stands, faces audience.*
	Come Sta.
GROUP FIVE:	Come Sta.
CHILD FIVE:	My name is Bruno. I come from Italy.
GROUP FIVE:	*Stand, form a circle with Bruno, march around saying:*

Isn't it fun
To meet someone different.
Isn't it fun
To make new friends.
Isn't it fun
To say to someone
"My name is...
Let's be friends."

Stand, say to audience.

My name is...

ALL:	LET'S BE FRIENDS!

NOVEMBER: *Remembrance Day*

Our Remembrance Day Service

Children take part as Veterans, Soldiers, Nurses, Family, Drummer, and Chorus. Two baskets of flowers and a wreath are placed at center.

SOLDIERS   VETERANS   CHORUS   NURSES   FAMILY   DRUMMER

DRUMMER: *Enters left, beats drum four times*

To the tune of "Land of Hope and Glory,"
Chorus enter in two lines. Veterans and
Soldiers enter left; Nurses and Family enter right.

CHORUS: The eleventh of November
It is Remembrance Day.
Americans remember too
They call it Veterans' Day.
On that day
In nineteen eighteen
Of peace everlasting
Men dared to dream.

DRUMMER: *Beats drum four times.*

VETERANS: On Remembrance Day we think
Of those who died.
Will you remember?

CHORUS: We will remember.

SOLDIERS: We honor their youth
And courage and pride.
Will you remember?

CHORUS: We will remember.

NURSES: We join our flowers
In a tribute small.
Will you remember?

CHORUS: We will remember.

FAMILY: We say a prayer
God bless them all.
Will you remember?

CHORUS: We will remember.

DRUMMER: *Beats drum four times.*

As the tape of "The Last Post" is played, the Chorus, in pairs, followed by the Veterans and Nurses, and the Soldiers and Family, all in pairs, move forward. Each takes a flower, places it on the wreath, and exits left and right, heads bowed.

DRUMMER: *Marches off, beating drum slowly.*

DECEMBER: *Christmas*

Christmas Cake

Let's all make
A Christmas Cake
Stir it well
'Til it's ready to bake
Eggs and butter
Peel, sultanas
Currants, raisins
Cherries, almonds
Grate the nutmeg
Mix the flour
Add the milk
Stir it round
Heat the oven
Line the tin
Is everything ready?
Let baking begin!

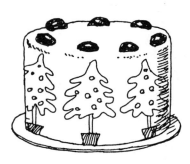

Christmas Bells

Ding-dong
Christmas Day

Ding-dong
Santa's sleigh

Ding-dong
Christmas Tree

Ding-dong
Toys for me

Ding-dong
Bells ringing

Ding-dong
Carol-singing

Ding-dong
Calls to make

Ding-dong
Christmas cake

Ding-dong
Candlelight

Ding-dong
Good night

Christmas Play

All the children
From grade three down
Are on the bus
And off to town.
They'll have a simply
Lovely time
They're going to a
Christmas play.
The bus pulls up
And out they file
Into the theatre
And down the aisle.
They find their seats
They settle in
The lights go down
The show begins.

Christmas Decorations

Silver tinsel
Holly green
A shining star
On the Christmas tree.

Paper chains
Of gold and red
And mistletoe
Hung overhead.

Christmas lanterns
In a row
Lighted candles
Softly glow.

The house is dressed
In decorations
For its Christmas
Celebrations.

A Christmas Rhyme

Christmas is giving
Christmas is sharing
Christmas is loving
Christmas is caring

Christmas Stocking

Christmas stocking
Round and fat
Bulging full
Of this and that.

Christmas stocking
Stuffed with toys
Some for all the
Girls and boys.

Christmas stocking
Bright and red
Waiting for me
By my bed.

Christmas stocking
Once a year
Bringing us our
Christmas cheer.

DECEMBER: *Christmas*

A Nativity Play

Mary and Joseph enter left. Mary, carrying baby, sits on a stool behind cradle, at center. Joseph stands behind.

ANGELS:	*Enter left.* Angels are in Bethlehem To see the little Child Lying in His mother's arms Sleeping meek and mild.
ALL:	Baby Jesus, we love you.
SHEPHERDS:	*Enter right.* Shepherds left their fields that night They travelled long and far Until they found a stable And saw the door ajar.
ALL:	Baby Jesus, we love you.
LAMBS:	*Enter left.* Little lambs following Their masters through the snow Came upon the stable And trotted in, tiptoe.
ALL:	Baby Jesus, we love you.
COWS:	*Enter right.* Around the manger stood the cows Gazing on the scene A baby lay among the hay It seemed to them a dream.
ALL:	Baby Jesus, we love you.
DONKEY:	*Enter left.* Quietly in a corner A patient donkey stood He'd carried Mary many miles As gently as he could.
ALL:	Baby Jesus, we love you.
WISE MEN:	*Enter right.* Bringing gifts, three wise men came Following a star It led them to a stable In a dark inn yard.
ALL:	Baby Jesus, we love you.
ALL:	As angels watched and gently smiled On Mary and the sleeping child All inside the stable there Bowed their heads and said a prayer.
	Baby Jesus, we love you.

JANUARY: *Children's Book Week*

Caring for a Book

I am a book.
I am shiny and new.
I'd like to be read
By someone like you.

Look at my cover.
It's very strong.
But treat it well
Or it won't last long.

Please turn my pages
With special care
Slowly gently
Then I won't tear.

You'll like my pictures
So have a good look
But please don't scribble
On this little book.

I like to be shared
So find a friend
And read me together
Right to the end.

My home is on
The library rack
So when I am finished
Please put me back.

That's an important
Thing to do
Then other children
Can read me too.

Choosing a Book

The scene is a child's bedroom. A bed is placed center stage. Mother and child enter. Mother tucks child in bed.

MOTHER: Which story would you like me to read you tonight, Simon?

SIMON: I can't choose, Mom. There are so many.

MOTHER: You think about it. I'll be back in a few minutes. *(exits)*

Simon lies down, Peter Rabbit's group enters.

PETER RABBIT:
(holding storybook)
I'm Peter Rabbit
How do you do?
You'll get to know me well.
I've two tall ears
And a fluffy tail.
I've lots of stories to tell.

PETER'S GROUP:
Please take me down
From the library shelf
And share my adventures too.
I hope you enjoy reading me.
I'd like to be read by you.

Doctor Dolittle's group enters.

DR. DOLITTLE:
(holding storybook)
Doctor Dolittle
Is my name.
I talk "Animal Talk"
Like "Chicken Peeps"
And "Pussy Meows"
And "Lion and Tiger Roar."

DR. DOLITTLE'S GROUP:
Please take me down
From the library shelf
And share my adventures too.
I hope you enjoy reading me.
I'd like to be read by you.

Wild Thing's group enters.

WILD THING:
(holding storybook)
Have you heard
Of the Wild Things?
We belong to Max, our King.
We gnash our teeth, we sharpen our claws.
We're terribly Wild Things.

WILD THING'S GROUP:
Please take me down
From the library shelf
And share my adventures too.
I hope you enjoy reading me.
I'd like to be read by you.

Christopher Robin's group enters.

CHRISTOPHER ROBIN:
(holding storybook)
Christopher Robin
Is my name.
This is my friend, Pooh Bear.
Piglet and Eeyore

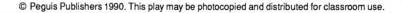

Are my friends too
But Pooh is always there.

CHRISTOPHER'S GROUP: Please take me down
From the library shelf
And share my adventures too.
I hope you enjoy reading me.
I'd like to be read by you.

Very Hungry Caterpillar's group enters.

VERY HUNGRY CATERPILLAR *(holding storybook)* I'm the Very Hungry
Cat - er - pill - ar.
I eat and eat all day,
Pears and leaves
Strawberries and cheese.
My favorite is chocolate cake.

CATERPILLAR'S GROUP: Please take me down
From the library shelf
And share my adventures too.
I hope you enjoy reading me.
I'd like to be read by you.

Captain Hook's group enters.

CAPTAIN HOOK: *(holding storybook)* I'm a pirate.
I'm Captain Hook.
Enemy of Peter Pan.
I'm wicked and fierce
And evil and bold
I'll do you in if I can.

HOOK'S GROUP: Please take me down
From the library shelf
And share my adventures too.
I hope you enjoy reading me.
I'd like to be read by you.

DR. SEUSS: *(holding storybook)* I'm Dr. Seuss
I like to write books
Green Eggs and Ham
The Cat in the Hat
And lots of stories
Just like that!

DR. SEUSS' GROUP: Please take me down
From the library shelf
And share my adventures too.
I hope you enjoy reading me.
I'd like to be read by you.

Simon falls asleep. Mother enters.

MOTHER: Simon, have you decided which
story you would like?

ALL *(whisper)* There are lots of books
For you to read
Upon the library shelf.
Have a good look.
Take your time.
Then just help yourself.

FEBRUARY: *Valentine's Day*

A Special Day for Emily

Emily was new to school.
She felt quite lonely
And strange and blue.
But Emily's teacher
Understood
As Emily'd rather hoped
He would.
He sat her with
A new friend, Jane
And Emily soon stopped
Feeling strange.
She'd come back to school
On a special day
The fourteenth of February—
Valentine's Day.
Her teacher showed her
A box he'd made.
"It's our classroom mail box,"
He explained.
"We made valentine cards
At school last week
And mailed them
In this box you see.
It's William's turn
To deliver mail today.

He'll start his deliveries
Right away."
Emily thought to herself,
"What a good game to play
And what lovely cards
Are on display.
If only I had
Been at school
I could have made
A valentine too."
William had
Only one card left.
"Emily this is yours,"
He said.
She was so surprised.
She felt quite shy,
She opened the card
And read inside…
"To Emily
Welcome to our school.
Happy Valentine's Day
To you
With love from everyone
In grade two."

MARCH OR APRIL: *Easter*

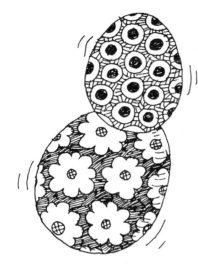

Easter Egg

I like to look at my Easter Egg
Dressed in silver and gold.

I like to feel my Easter Egg,
Oval, smooth, and cold.

I like to smell my Easter Egg
Chocolate-sweet and rich.

I like to hear my Easter Egg
Crack into little bits.

And now I'll eat my Easter Egg
I can hardly wait
I'd better eat it before it melts
I hope I'm not too late.

The Meaning of Easter

It was the Thursday before Easter. The Jones children looked forward to Easter every year. And this year they had made something special to give to their mother and father on Easter Sunday. Their teacher had shown them how to decorate eggs in pretty patterns and package them in little baskets made of gold and silver paper. The Jones children had hidden their presents in a secret place ready for Easter Sunday.

The Jones children lived on a farm in the country. There was always a lot of work to do on the farm. One of the children's jobs was to feed the hens and gather the eggs, and to make sure that the mother hens, who were sitting on their nests waiting for their eggs to hatch, had plenty of food and water.

The Jones children were very fond of the mother hens. They even had pet names for them. Each morning the children greeted the hens, saying, "Good Morning, Jenny," (or Matilda or Clementine), and the mother hens would cluck-cluck, "Good Morning," back.

But the Jones children were not very fond of the roosters. Some of them were quite fierce. All except one. He was a gentle old bird. The children called him Bernard.

Bernard was really old. Even his voice was old. When he tried to crow each morning his thin old voice sounded like an old cracked gramophone record. He walked very slowly and he had lost quite a few of his black tail feathers.

But Bertha, who was one of the mother hens, loved Bernard and they often spent the day together looking for worms in the vegetable garden under the apple tree.

Now the next day was Good Friday. When the Jones children woke up they knew that something was different. What could it be? Then they knew they had not heard Bernard's old reedy voice crowing from the farmyard.

The children went into the kitchen for breakfast, and Mr. Jones came in from the yard. "Don't be upset," he said gently to the children, "Dear old Bernard has died. I have just found him."

Of course the children were upset. Bernard had been one of the farmyard family for such a long time.

After a little while the Jones children started to think about Bernard's funeral. They decided to bury him in his favorite spot, under the apple tree. Mr. Jones made a little wooden cross and helped the children to carve BERNARD ROOSTER, R.I.P. on a flat stone to mark the grave. They dug a hole under the apple tree and Mrs. Jones put a little bunch of flowers on the grave.

Then they wrapped Bernard in a piece of white sheet and put him very gently in a cardboard box Mrs. Jones had given them. Then they carried him out to the little grave, and Mr. Jones buried him and placed the cross firmly in the ground and rested the headstone against it, and the children put the little bunch of flowers on the grave.

Good Friday was a sad day. On Saturday while the Jones children were doing their jobs, they saw that the flowers on Bernard's grave were drooping badly, so Mrs. Jones gave them a pretty little glass jar and some more flowers, and they put the little jar of flowers on the grave. Then they went on with their jobs.

The next day was Easter Sunday, the day to give their parents the special Easter eggs they had made.

Mother and Father were just delighted with their eggs. They thought their children were very clever indeed. They put the Easter eggs in their little baskets on the mantlepiece over the fireplace so that everyone could see them.

Then Mrs. Jones went to her secret hiding place under the sink to fetch the children's Easter eggs. As she did so she looked out of the kitchen window.

"Look, children," she cried. There was Bertha Hen with her family of new chickens, standing under the apple tree looking at Bernard's grave.

"Look at that little chicken with the black feathers," said Mr. Jones to the children, "does he remind you of someone?"

The Jones children looked at the chicken very carefully. Of course—he looked just like Bernard.

"Even his feathers are black like Bernard's," said the children.

"Shall we call that little black chicken 'Bernard'?" asked Mrs. Jones.

"Oh yes, let's," cried the children. "Bernard would like that."

Then Mrs. Jones took the Easter eggs from the secret hiding place and gave them to the children. They were delicious chocolate eggs wrapped in bright shiny paper. The Jones children loved them.

"Why do we give each other eggs at Easter?" they asked their parents.

"It's a custom people have," said their father.

"Yes," said Mother, "Our little chickens hatch out of their eggs to start a new life in the farmyard, don't they? So we give Easter eggs as a sign of new life, so people can feel happy and have something to look forward to."

"We are looking forward to eating our Easter eggs," said the Jones children.

And they did. And the Easter eggs were delicious!

APRIL OR MAY: *The Stanley Cup*

What Is the Stanley Cup?

We know we're only
In grade one
And everyone says,
"You are too young."
But when something's happening
Round about
We simply hate
To be left out.

It's in the papers
It's on TV
We'd like to know
What does it mean?
Our father knows
And so does our mother
And so does our sister
And so does our brother.

What is everyone
Talking about?
They get so excited
They start to shout.
Grandfather says it's a
Grownups' party
Then he laughs at us
So we really don't know.

It could be a new kind of
Ice cream or food.
Perhaps it's a game
We don't know, do you?
Is it a drink
Like a special milkshake?
Or a piece of china
From outer space?

We're not too young.
We're nearly six.
If we're not told soon
We may get sick.
Will some kind person
Please answer our queries
And tell us, "What is
The Stanley Cup?

MAY: *Mother's Day*

Mother's Day

The scene is mother's bedroom.
Mother is in bed asleep, stage center.
Children tiptoe in, form five groups in a
semi-circle behind mother.

CHILDREN: *Point to mother, fingers on lips, whisper.*

                   MOTHER'S DAY

GROUP ONE: It's getting near
                   It's almost here
                   That very special
                   Day of the year.

                   It's always in
                   The month of May
                   Of course, you've guessed
                   It's Mother's Day.

GROUP TWO: A special day
                   We keep for mothers
                   Not fathers or sisters
                   Or babies or brothers.

                   It belongs to Mother
                   It's hers alone
                   One day in the year
                   For her very own.

GROUP THREE:

We'll get up early
While she's asleep
And into the kitchen
We'll softly creep.

We'll make some toast
And a pot of tea
And set her tray
So carefully.

GROUP FOUR:

We'll write in her card
We made it ourselves
We'll need to pick
Some flowers as well.

Fresh from the store
A pretty bouquet
Of chrysanthemums
For Mother's Day.

A girl carrying card and flowers, and a boy carrying a tray enter, followed by Father.

We'll carry the tray
Into her room
She's fast asleep
But she'll wake up soon.

GROUP FIVE:

We'll give her a kiss
And then we'll say
"A very happy
Mother's Day."

Mother wakes.

(*If mothers are present, children blow kisses to their mothers and repeat the last verse.)

ALL:

We'll give *you* a kiss
And then we'll say
"A very happy
Mother's Day."

JUNE: *Arbor Day*

A Tree's Story

CHARACTERS:	Storyteller, Tree, Bird, Squirrel, Snake, Bees, Three Men.
SCENE:	In the forest, a large tree, formed by children standing and sitting at different levels, stands in the center.
STORYTELLER:	*Enter right.*
	In the beginning There was a tree.
TREE:	I am the tree, I am the tree.
STORYTELLER:	And the tree was The home of the bird.
	Bird enters left, flutters around the tree.
BIRD:	I am the bird, I am the bird.
STORYTELLER:	And the tree was The home of the squirrel.
	Squirrel enters right, runs around the tree.
SQUIRREL:	I am the squirrel, I am the squirrel.
STORYTELLER:	And the tree was The home of the snake.
	Snake enters left, wriggles around the tree.
SNAKE:	I am the snake, I am the snake.
STORYTELLER:	And the tree was The home of the bees.
	Bees enter right, fly around the tree.
BEES:	We are the bees, We are the bees.
	Creatures shelter under the tree and look up into the branches.
CREATURES:	The tree is our home. We love our tree.
STORYTELLER:	Then one day Along came...
	Three men enter left. They carry axes. Creatures huddle in fear.

1st MAN:	We've come far enough. Let's have a rest now. Which of these trees Do you want to chop down?
2nd MAN:	I need some wood For my barbeque. That tree over there... That one will do.

He points to the creatures' tree.

3rd MAN:	My wife would say If she were here, "That tree has grown there For a hundred years."

Other men nod. They sit down and eat their lunches.

BIRD:	They can't take our tree.
SQUIRREL:	They can't take our home.
SNAKE:	We'll have to do something.
ALL:	But we're all alone.
BEES:	Do not fear We bees are here. We will protect you Have no fear.

Men fall asleep.

BEES:	We'll fight for our lives Our tree will survive But first we must get OR-GAN-IZED!

Bees scurry behind tree, looking busy. They emerge carrying "SAVE OUR TREE" signs. They give three signs to the others. All stand guarding the tree.)

TREE:

It doesn't take long
To chop down a tree,
Just as long as a song
Or a fairy story.

It doesn't take long
To banish cool shade,
The cows in the field
Are the ones who'll pay.

It doesn't take long
Not long at all
For a beautiful tree
To shudder then fall.

Tree and creatures bow their heads. Men wake up.

1st MAN:

I thought I heard something
In the trees
Like the whistling of birds
Or the rustle of leaves.

2nd MAN:

You know, I've been thinking
Of what your wife said,
I won't burn wood logs
I'll use gas instead.

3rd MAN:

Perhaps you are right
We should leave the trees
I wouldn't harm mine
In my garden at home.

Men exit left.

STORYTELLER:

In the beginning
There was a tree.

TREE:

Lifts head.

I am the tree
I am the tree.

CREATURES:

Lift heads.

The tree is our home
We love our tree.

ALL:
(slowly)

Though we're safe for today
We will wait and see
What tomorrow may bring
To the life of our tree.

JUNE: *Father's Day*

Fathers

What are fathers
Made of?
What are fathers
Made of?
TV news
Trips to zoos,
That's what fathers
Are made of.

What are fathers
Made of?
What are fathers
Made of?
Lending an ear
And drying a tear,
That's what fathers
Are made of.

What are fathers
Made of?
What are fathers
Made of?
Helpful smiles
Driving miles,
That's what fathers
Are made of.

What are fathers
Made of?
What are fathers
Made of?
Shorts and thongs
Jokes and songs,
That's what fathers
Are made of.

What are fathers
Made of?
What are fathers
Made of?
Smiles and frowns
Ups and downs,
That's what fathers
Are made of.

What are fathers
Made of?
What are fathers
Made of?
Tickling fights
And flying kites,
That's what fathers
Are made of.

What are fathers
Made of?
What are fathers
Made of?
Comfort and care
And being there,
That's what fathers
Are made of.

What are fathers
Made of?
What are fathers
Made of?
Baseball scores
And gardening chores,
That's what fathers
Are made of.

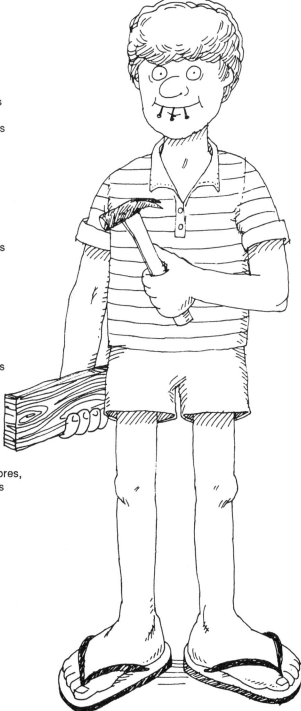

JUNE: *Keep Our Parks Beautiful*

Litterbug

Enter Mr. Sign, left, carrying placard "Don't Litter the Beach". Enter Mr. Bin, right, wearing label "Litter Bin."

MR. SIGN:	Good Morning, Mr. Bin.
MR. BIN:	Good Morning, Mr. Sign. Can you see my label?
MR. SIGN:	Can you read my sign?
MR. SIGN AND MR. BIN:	Drop the litter in Drop the litter in Drop the litter in And feed the litter bin.

Enter children; first group skips eight steps left in a semi-circle.

FIRST GROUP:	Here we are At the park today It's fun to be On holiday.

Second group skips eight steps right to form a circle with the first group.

SECOND GROUP:	We have come To have some fun Let's play here And share the sun.

Children play in a circle. Litterbugs enter left.

LITTERBUGS: *(shout)*	We are dirty We are mean We don't like The parks to be clean.

Litterbugs march about, dropping litter.

LITTERBUGS:

Drop it here
Drop it there
Litter, litter
Everywhere!

Children sit up, see litter.

CHILDREN:
(in horror)

Litter here
Litter there
Litter, litter
Everywhere!

MR. SIGN AND MR. BIN:
(weeping)

Litter here
Litter there
Litter, litter
We despair.

Children skip about, picking up litter.

CHILDREN:

Clean the park
So we can play
Pick it up
It's in the way.

MR. SIGN AND MR. BIN:
(smiling)

Drop it in
Drop it in
Drop it in
And feed the Bin.

Children place litter in bin.

CHILDREN:

Now the park
Is nice and clean
Litter's nowhere
To be seen.

LITTERBUGS:
(whisper)

We are dirty
We are mean
We don't like
The parks to be clean.

Children shoo Litterbugs off stage.

CHILDREN:

Goodbye, Litterbugs
Off with you
Take your litter
With you too.

Litterbugs slink off. Children, Mr. Sign and Mr. Bin skip in a circle.

CHILDREN
MR. SIGN AND MR. BIN:

Litter now is
Cleaned away
Litterbugs sent
Upon their way.
What good work
We've done today
Now let's have
Our holiday.

JUNE: *Fair Day*

A Fair of Their Own

Every year the teachers at Roleystone Elementary School take their children to the Autumn Fair.

On the Monday after the fair some of the children were talking to Mrs. Fleming, the school principal.

"Do other places have fairs too, Mrs. Fleming?" asked a grade two student.

"Oh, yes, Stuart," said Mrs. Fleming, and she told the children all about fairs in other places.

"Could we have a fair of our own, right here in the playground?" asked one of the boys in grade three.

"Yes, we could, Ying," said Mrs. Fleming.

"Oh, that would be fun," said the children.

And that's just what happened.

Roleystone Elementary School decided to have a fair of its own.

Everyone was really excited.

They had to decide when to hold their fair, and where and how.

They had to plan how to fit everything in the playground, so they made a map.

They printed lots of little fair maps and made them into invitations to give to their parents.

They painted posters to display in shop windows.

They made hand-bills advertising the fair and put them in mailboxes. They prepared an advertisement for the local paper telling about the fair.

They made fair bags out of recycled bags and started to collect bottle tops to make into money tokens.

They printed labels and signs which showed where everything was.

They made little vases and bowls in their art classes to sell on Fair Day.

They painted murals and pictures, and made mobiles and puppets and masks, and knit wool into little scarves, and stitched little pictures using thread and wool.

All these lovely things were to be displayed in the arts and crafts exhibition.

They prepared a vegetable garden and grew vegetables for the horticultural display.

They collected seeds and grew them in little pots for the potted plant stall.

They made jam and cookies and cake and iced tea and lemonade to sell on Fair Day.

They collected books and toys and old records and china for the Jumble Sale stall.

They cooked fruit cakes and planned how they would decorate them for the cake-judging competition.

They asked a local police officer to help with the road safety display, and they practiced riding their bicycles for the bicycle safety demonstration.

They made sure there were plenty of containers of water for the animals on Fair Day, and at home they groomed their pets ready for the grand parade and the pet show.

Children who owned puppies and kittens and guinea pigs and chickens prepared them for display in the animal nursery. Each class practiced its item for the concert on the front lawn.

Grade one had decided to sing some animal songs, grade two to play rhythm band selections, and grade three to recite some poems they had made up about the School Fair Day.

At last the great day arrived.

The fair started at nine o'clock, and soon the playground was filled with families and friends.

The grand parade was a splendid sight.

The brownie and cub packs led off, followed by the children with their pets, and they all marched around the school playground to the music of the scout band.

Everyone enjoyed the day.

At assembly on Monday morning Mrs. Fleming spoke to the children.

"Our very own Fair Day was such a success that we will have one every year," she said. "It was very hard work, but it was worth it."

All the children agreed. They could hardly wait for next year!

Part Three

Poems and Stories
for Classroom Themes

OURSELVES: *At School*

First Day at School

It's my first day at school today.
I look around and see
Everyone else's faces
Looking back at me.

It's my first day at school today.
I've a desk that's just for me.
I'll keep my books and pencils
As tidy as can be.

It's my first day at school today.
They're so many things to see.
Puppets and paints and a budgie
And books for me to read.

It's my first day at school today.
I'm busy as can be
Stories and songs and printing
And a teddy bear stamp for me.

It's my first day at school today.
My teacher is smiling at me.
"Please help me feed the fish," she says,
"Let's do it carefully."

It's my first day at school today.
I'm painting a picture of me.
I'll take it with me when I go home
To show the family.

It's my first day at school today.
I'm tired as can be.
But I've had a lovely time today.
And there's Mommy waiting for me!

A Sharing Song

(To the tune of "Twinkle Twinkle Little Star.")

Hello, hello, how are you?
Let's join in for a minute or two.
We all have some things to share.
We're all friends and we all care.
Stand up, chair in, please don't chat.
Tiptoe quietly to the mat.

A Storytime Song

(To the tune of "Mary Had a Little Lamb.")

Now it's time for storytime
Storytime, storytime
Now it's time for storytime
Come and sit by me.

Open up the storybook
Storybook, storybook
Open up the storybook
Which story will it be?

A Classroom Walk

Put on your magic glasses
And come for a walk with me.
Look carefully in this corner
And tell me what you see.
(reading center))

Now here is something interesting
Whatever can it be?
It's a table, with some things on it.
Tell me what you see.
(interest table)

If you like songs or stories
Or puppets or TV,
Sit on our magic carpet
And tell me what you see.
(mat area)

If you walk a little further
You'll find something else with me.
This is a very special place.
Tell me what you see.
(house center)

And look what I've found over here.
It's as tidy as can be.
I'm sure it's very useful.
Tell me what you see.
(storage unit—cupboards)

I'll stop walking for a minute
Because I really want to see
This great big empty pin-up board.
Tell me what you see.
(bulletin board)

I've had a lovely classroom walk.
I'm glad you came with me.
But I'm sure we left some places out
So tell me what you see.

OURSELVES: *At School*

Learning Our Names

"Good morning, everyone," said Miss Fitzharding to her grade ones on their first day at school.

"My name is Miss Fitzharding," she told them, "and now we are going to learn your names."

She brought the children out onto the mat and sat them in a big circle.

"What is your name?" she asked the little boy sitting next to her.

"My name is Davie," he told her.

"Would you help me to sing a song please, Davie?" asked Miss Fitzharding. And Davie said he would.

Then Miss Fitzharding sang a name-game to the children.

It had the same tune as "Mary had a Little Lamb."

> We would like to
> Know your name
> Know your name
> Know your name
> Will you please
> Tell us your name?

Miss Fitzharding stopped singing and smiled at Davie.

"Davie is my name," he said.

"Davie is your name," sang Miss Fitzharding.

Then everyone joined in singing the name-game song.

CHILDREN:	We would like to
	Know your name
	Know your name
	Know your name
	Will you please
	Tell us your name?
DAVIE:	Davie is my name.
CHILDREN:	Davie is your name.

"Now we all know Davie's name," said Miss Fitzharding. "It is a nice name."

"It is my grandfather's name too," said Davie.

"That *is* interesting, Davie," said Miss Fitzharding.

Then they all sang the name-game song again.

This time Miss Fitzharding asked Misty to help them sing the song.

CHILDREN:	We would like to
	Know your name
	Know your name
	Know your name
	Will you please
	Tell us your name?
MISTY:	Misty is my name.
CHILDREN:	Misty is your name.

"Now we all know Misty's name," said Miss Fitzharding, "It is a pretty name."

"It's the name of my Daddy's favorite song," said Misty.

"That *is* interesting, Misty," said Miss Fitzharding.

It was Sally's turn next, then Li's, then Ricardo's.

Now we know the names of five children," said Miss Fitzharding. "When we come in from play we'll learn some more of your names."

How did *you* learn the names of the children in *your* class?

← BERTIE GERM

Our Health Rules

Our teacher likes us
Neat and clean.
We each have a health bag.
Mine is green.

I have a pink comb
To keep my hair neat
And a little striped towel
Mommy washes each week.

And some soap in my bag
For my hands and my face
And a yellow toothbrush
In a red plastic case.

I have some kleenex
And some band-aids too.
They fit in my plastic case
But there isn't much room!

We wash after play
Our hands and our faces
We all comb our hair
And tie our shoelaces.

When we've eaten lunch
Our teeth we clean.
The front, the back,
And in-between.

We try to follow
Our health rules each day
So our whole class can keep
Bertie Germ away.

OURSELVES: *At School*

Weather Rhymes

Marching

I am the sun
Am I yellow or red?
Watch out for my fire
When I shine on your head.

Circling

I am the snow
Swirly and free
If I turn into ice
Don't slip on me.

Swaying

I am a cloud
Floaty and white
If I turn black
There'll be showers tonight.

Creeping

I am the fog
I cling and I crawl
I creep down the street
And through your front door.

Running

I am the rain
On your windowpane
You can't do without me
So don't complain!

Skipping

I am the wind
You can't see me
But I'm very strong
So make use of me.

Fiz-Ed

It happened after
Morning play
We'd only been
At school two days
When suddenly
Our teacher said
"Now it's time
To do FIZ-ED."

FIZ-ED? FIZ-ED
What was FIZ-ED?
But, "Down to the gym,"
Was all she said.
A man stood there
He looked quite nice
"Hello," he said.
"I'm Mr. Bryce."

Then off with our socks
And sandals and shoes
For the next half-hour
We had plenty to do
Games with hoops
And ropes and balls
We had great fun
We enjoyed it all.

Mr. Bryce
Gave us a rest
He chatted to us
While we dressed
We decided to ask him,
"Please sir," we said,
"What we just did,
Was that FIZ-ED?"

Our Art Teacher

Miss Shepherd lives in room 16
She likes us all to keep it clean.

Miss Shepherd's hair is long and brown
Sometimes it's up, sometimes it's down.

Miss Shepherd wears such pretty things
Like butterfly combs and silver rings.

Miss Shepherd's nails are really long
Her fingers are thin, but they're very strong.

Miss Shepherd's voice is always soft
She's very quiet, but she smiles a lot.

Miss Shepherd says, "Please bring with you
Your painting smocks and smiling faces too."

Miss Shepherd's room is like a nest
It's one of the places we like best.

Miss Shepherd has paints, and clay, and glue
She thinks up lovely things to do.

Miss Shepherd just smiles when she hears me say,
"I wish we did art every day."

OURSELVES: *At School*

Our Birthday Ceremony

The grade ones were having a lovely time.

They were making birthday cakes.

The cakes were not made of eggs and flour and milk and sugar.

They were made of cardboard and paint and gold and silver paper and any other odds and ends the grade ones could find in Miss Adamson's recycle box.

There were twelve birthday cakes, one for each month of the year.

The children whose birthdays were in January made the January cake, the February-birthday children made the February cake and so on.

When the cakes were finished Miss Adamson pinned them up.

They looked beautiful.

Each one was different.

Miss Adamson printed the children's names on labels and stapled them under the birthday cakes, so that everyone could see when his or her birthday was.

From then on when anyone had a birthday, the class held a little birthday ceremony for him or her.

So that the children whose birthdays were in July and August didn't miss out, the first birthday ceremony was for them. Here it is.

  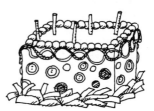

Birthdays

Teacher places a mock birthday cake on her table and lights the candles.

A birthday for you?
A birthday for me?
A birthday for SOMEONE
Now who can it be?

Birthday child responds, moves to table.

A birthday's very special.
We'd like to share it too.
So let's all sing together
A birthday song for you.

Children sing "Happy Birthday"; child blows out the candles; tells class about his birthday.

Our Librarian

Our librarian stands behind her desk.
She smiles at me and says, "Hello."
She takes my books, and finds my cards,
She's never cross, though I'm so slow.
SHE KNOWS EVERYTHING ABOUT BOOKS!

It's very hard to find a book.
I like to look and take my time.
She always helps. "You might like this,"
She tells me with a smile.
SHE KNOWS EVERYTHING ABOUT BOOKS!

And when at last I've chosen one
She stamps the dates so straight and neat
To remind me when my book is due
"Enjoy your book," she says to me.
SHE KNOWS EVERYTHING ABOUT BOOKS!

OURSELVES: *At Home*

"Family Voices"

Benjamin was tired. Mr. Carter, the scoutmaster, had taken the boys for a long hike. It had been great fun, but now Benjamin was ready for bed. As he was going to sleep he heard Dad say,

> "Gas prices, gas prices,
> Gas prices, gas prices."

Dad was reading the paper in the kitchen. Grandfather pretended to listen politely, but he was mumbling to himself,

> "Roses, tulips, daffodils, daisies,
> Roses, tulips, daffodils, daisies."

Benjamin knew Grandfather was planning next year's garden. Grandmother pretended to listen politely, but she was whispering to herself,

> "Jam tarts, cream puffs,
> Jam tarts, cream puffs."

Benjamin knew Grandmother was thinking about tomorrow night's dessert. Mother pretended to listen politely, but she was saying, over and over to herself,

> "Cereal, cereal, cereal, cereal,
> Cereal, cereal, cereal, cereal,"

Benjamin knew Mother was working out her shopping list. She always forgot the cereal.
Then Auntie Joan and Uncle Jeff arrived.

> "Newspaper, newspaper,
> Newspaper, newspaper,"

chattered Auntie Joan.

> "Par five, par five,
> Par five, par five,"

boasted Uncle Jeff.

"Oh dear," thought Benjamin, "I'll never get to sleep."

> "Gas prices, Gas prices,
> Gas prices, Gas prices,
> Roses, tulips, daffodils, daisies,
> Roses, tulips, daffodils, daisies,
> Jam tarts, cream puffs,
> Jam tarts, cream puffs,
> Cereal, cereal, cereal, cereal,
> Cereal, cereal, cereal, cereal,
> Newspaper, newspaper,
> Newspaper, newspaper,
> Par five, par five,
> Par five, par five."

At last they all went home. Dad put Whiskers, the cat, out for the night. Mother looked at her shopping list.
"Now, what have I forgotten?" she said to herself.
"Cereal, Mom," called Benjamin drowsily.

Timmy's Treasures

Mother stood
At the bedroom door.
She'd a look on her face
Timmy'd seen before.
"Look at this stuff
Lying about,
Timmy, please come
And sort things out."
Timmy knew Mother
Meant what she said.
He'd much prefer
To be playing instead.
But he found some treasures,
While doing his chore,
And as he kept working
He found lots more.
A jar of marbles,
Some comic books,
His old harmonica,
A tin of fish hooks,
A model plane
With a broken wing,
A telephone
Made of tins and string.

He hadn't played
With these things for years,
He'd completely forgotten
That they were here.
There were his stamps
And his trusty scout knife.
He was really having
The time of his life.
Finding his treasures
Was such fun.
Before he knew it
The job was done.
Then Mother came
To the bedroom door.
She took one look
At the mess on the floor.
"Timmy," she said,
"Have you sorted things out?
I'll take all this stuff
And throw it out."
Timmy tried to say,
"Please don't throw it away."

Mother took no notice
In her haste.
But then she saw
The look on his face.
She sat down slowly
On Timmy's bed,
"Treasures are precious,"
Was all she said.
Timmy smiled
And nodded his head.
Then he and Mother
Found a storage place.
A nice big cupboard
With plenty of space
To keep Timmy's treasures
Where they'd be safe.
He packed everything in
As neat as could be
And Mother said
As she gave him the key,
"You've learned something new
Today, Timmy,
It's called "Re-spons-i-bil-i-ty."

Anthea's Playhouse

In the back garden
Under a willow tree
Anthea's Daddy built a playhouse
As magic as can be.

Anthea's playhouse
Is her own little home
To share with her friends
Or be on her own.

She keeps it clean
With a little straw broom.
It's a dear little house
And there's plenty of room.

You may be tall
Like Auntie Fran
But you can fit in
You really can.

Anthea's house
Has a little front door
And a pointy roof
And a mat on the floor.

And a tiny porch
Where she sits in the sun
And has a rest
When her playing is done.

Mommy gave Anthea
Some flowers in a pot
To grow and take care of
And water when it's hot.

Inside her house
There's a table and chairs
Where her dollies have lunch
With her teddy bears.

There's a little pine dresser
With cups and plates
And a little teapot
And a tin for cake.

One day Anthea
Might ask us to tea.
We'd love to visit
Her home in the tree.

OURSELVES: *At Home*

José's Bedroom

José's bedroom was next to his parents' bedroom. It was not a huge room exactly, but it was large enough for his bed to fit in, his toy cupboard, his bookcase, his desk and a chair, and his dresser.

It was a bit cluttered, but it looked lived in. José loved it. It was his special place.

He was particularly fond of his window. As his parents' house was quite old—about sixty years actually—his window was an old-fashioned window that opened outwards onto the garden. It was made of little squares of wood filled in with small panes of glass. Through his window José could see a thick, green creeper growing all over the side fence. It was José's private jungle.

On one wall of his bedroom, José's mother had painted a mural. There was a big green tree with a fluffy owl sitting in it, and a cheeky little bluebird flying about…There was a yellow path with a spotty dog and a grey elephant walking along it, and a toadstool and a little striped bee.

José's mother had made the curtains and a bedspread. The material had animals all over it too, the same animals as the mural had, except for a rabbit, but his grandparents had given him two little china rabbits, so that was all right.

José kept his favorite books on the top shelf of his bookcase and he kept his jigsaws and puzzles and games on the bottom shelf.

His teddy bear always slept on José's bed, and Kermit and Miss Piggy always sat on his desk.

José's father had given him a little flashlight which he kept on a small table beside his bed in case he needed it in the night. His cousin Sarah had given him a little alarm clock which he knew how to set (but not too early, his mother had warned him).

José's dresser had four drawers in it for his socks and underwear and sweaters, and his closet had plenty of hanging space for his jeans and jackets and shirts and raincoat.

He had a bulletin board on one wall and he stuck all sorts of things on it—pictures, drawings, maps, buttons, and the skeleton of a little fish he had found on the beach.

There was a special hiding place in his desk where he kept some old coins his grandfather had given him and a box full of tickets. José collected tickets. Whenever the family went on an outing—to the museum, on the ferry, to the zoo, to the football game, on a train ride, to the circus—José would save the tickets. He already had quite a large collection.

José had organized his bedroom carefully to allow quite a wide space between his desk and his bookcase. This was where he would store his guitar. His father said he could learn to play the guitar when he was old enough, so he kept that space empty, ready for when he had a guitar of his own.

José loved his bedroom. It was where he played with his friend, Billy. It was where his mother and father told him stories at bedtime. It was where he stayed in bed when he was sick. It was where he opened his presents on Christmas morning.

It was José's special place.

People We Know

People we know
People we know—
Let's say hello
To people we know.

The baker, the farmer,
The butcher, the dentist,
The police officer, the miner,
The firefighter, the chemist.

The engineer, the plumber,
The teacher, the chef,
The sailor, the soldier,
The mail carrier, the vet.

The nurse and the doctor,
The lifeguard too—
So many people—
I know them, do you?

People we know
People we know—
Let's say hello
To people we know.

People Who Help Us

Siren, engine, helmet, axe,
Hydrants, hoses, ladders, taps,
Puddles of water all about—
My job's done, the fire's out.
   (I'm a firefighter.)

I deliver all your letters
And perhaps a bill or two,
Receipts and invitations
And a birthday card for you.
   (I'm a mail carrier.)

When you ride your bike or walk to school,
I help you learn your safety rules,
If you're lost at the show, or can't find your way,
It's my job to help you, every day.
   (I'm a police officer.)

I stand on the beach
On fine sunny days.
I wait and I watch
You swim and play.
If you go out too far
Or start sinking, too
Just call out for me
I'll come to save you.
   (I'm a lifeguard.)

OURSELVES: *At Home*

Father Keeps House

Mr. Stanley worked in an office.
Mrs. Stanley worked in an office, too.

They lived in a small brick house with an orange tiled roof.
They had a big green lawn in the front, and a smaller one at the back.
They had two weeping willow trees and a bed of roses in front, and a greenhouse full of house plants around the side.
Mr. and Mrs. Stanley's house had three bedrooms, one for Mr. and Mrs. Stanley, and two extra bedrooms.
Mrs. Stanley was having a baby, so Mr. Stanley painted the second bedroom a pretty yellow color and Mrs. Stanley
    made some little white curtains with yellow flowers on them.
Mr. and Mrs. Stanley bought some baby things and put them in the baby's bedroom.

Mrs. Stanley had the baby. It was a little girl.
Mr. and Mrs. Stanley called her Susie. She was beautiful.

Mrs. Stanley was not very well when she came home from hospital.
The doctor said she had to stay in bed and rest.
Mrs. Stanley started to worry, but Mr. Stanley worked things out.

Mr. Stanley went to see his boss, and his boss said that Mr. Stanley could take his holidays so that he could look after
Mrs. Stanley and Susie.
And that's just what Mr. Stanley did.
> He learned to make the formula for Susie's bottle.
> He learned how to change diapers.
> He learned how to bathe the baby.
> He learned how to burp Susie after she'd had her bottle.
> He learned how to do the housework while Susie had her nap.
> He learned how to vacuum the floors with Susie strapped to his chest in her little papoose carrier.
> He took Susie to the doctor for her check-ups and injections.
> He took Susie to the gym when he did his work-outs and weight-lifting. She would lie in her carrier and
>   watch him.
All the men in the gym knew Susie and kootchie-cooed to her just like her mommy and daddy did at home.
Besides looking after Susie, Mr. Stanley did the washing and the cooking and the cleaning and the shopping and
    the gardening.

Slowly Mrs. Stanley grew stronger. The doctor was very pleased with her.
It was nearly time for Mr. Stanley to go back to work.
"You haven't had a holiday at all," said Mrs. Stanley, "You've spent it all looking after Susie and me."
But Mr. Stanley didn't mind a bit.

In fact…
That night Mr. and Mrs. Stanley had a long talk.
The next day Mr. Stanley rang up his boss.
He explained that he and Mrs. Stanley had both worked in offices…and…because Mrs. Stanley liked going to
    work…and Mr. Stanley liked staying home…Could he and Mrs. Stanley SHARE Mr. Stanley's job?
The boss thought very carefully. It was quite a new idea to him.
At last he said, "All right, we'll give it a try."

And that's just what happened.
Mr. and Mrs. Stanley shared Mr. Stanley's job and they shared being at home with Susie too.
Wasn't Susie a lucky little baby to have her mommy and daddy to share EVERYTHING with?

OURSELVES: *In the Neighborhood*

A Supermarket Story

The cash register on number six was very old. Almost worn out in fact. That was why he was on number six checkout, only six items at a time.

When he was younger he was known as Whizz Bang because he worked so efficiently.

> Ping ping ping ping
> Click
> Whizz bang!
> Ping ping ping ping
> Click
> Whizz bang!

The truth was, however, he had been overworked. He dreaded the supermarket opening each day. He dreaded the busy girl who pounded him from nine o'clock in the morning to half-past five each night. He knew that she knew that he was breaking down. He thought, "How much longer can I go on?"

> Ping ping ping ping
> Click
> Whizz bang!
> Ping ping ping ping
> Click
> Whizz bang!

But the busy girl had a soft spot for the old cash register. One day she said to the supermarket supervisor, "Dear old Whizz Bang needs a rest."

"Yes," said the supermarket supervisor, "any suggestions?"

"Well," said the busy girl, "I would like a new cash register."

"All right, it's the garbage dump for old Whizz Bang," said the supervisor.

Whizz Bang heard them. He really tried to work efficiently that day.

> Ping ping ping ping
> Click
> Whizz bang!
> Ping ping ping ping
> Click
> Whizz bang!

But it was no use. By three o'clock he was exhausted. Only one of his pings worked, and to make matters worse, the supervisor arrived with a brand new, shiny cash register for number six checkout. Whizz Bang was pushed to one side.

"I'll get rid of him tomorrow," said the supervisor.

"Excuse me," said a soft voice.

Whizz Bang was too upset to look, but he listened.

"Excuse me, but did I hear you say you were getting rid of this dear old cash register?"

"Oh, yes," said the supervisor cheerfully, "he's worn out."

OURSELVES: *In the Neighborhood*

The lady with the soft voice tapped Whizz Bang gently,

> Ping ping ping ping
> Click
> Whizz bang!
> Ping ping ping ping
> Click
> Whizz bang!

Whizz Bang was a bit slow, but he managed to work.

"I wonder," said the lady, "if you're going to get rid of him, could I buy him from you? We'd love to have him at our kindergarten."

"I'll see the manager, madam," said the supervisor.

When he came back, he nodded.

"The manager says there's no need to pay. We'll give him to your kindergarten. I'll get someone to take him out to your car."

"Oh, thank you," said the lady with the soft voice.

So Whizz Bang was taken to the kindergarten. The children were delighted to have him. They knew Whizz Bang was very old so they played with him very gently all the time. He was safe at last.

> Ping ping ping ping
> Click
> Whizz bang!
> Ping ping ping ping
> Click
> Whizz bang!

YM/YWCA

When David turned
Nine years of age
He decided to join
The YM/YWCA.

He told his friends
Ying and Kim
And they decided
To join with him.

They made new friends
They had games to play.
They really looked forward
To Saturdays.

David did workouts
At the gym
So did Ying
And so did Kim.

And best of all
The YM/YWCA
Held a camp
In the holidays.

No one got sick.
The weather stayed fine.
The friends all had
A marvellous time.

Putting up tents
Paddling canoes
Campfires, hikes
Chores to do.

David was glad
At nine years of age
He'd decided to join
The YM/YWCA.

Brownies

Anna is a brownie.
She wears a uniform.
A little brown dress
And an orange neck tie.
A little badge scarf
And a belt with a pouch
And a little brownie badge
She's careful not to slouch.

Anna loves powwows
And working on her badges
And brownie revels
And pack holidays.
Brownies always
Get jobs done.
A brownie's life
Is lots of fun.

Kindergarten

We're on our way to kindergarten
Although we're in grade one.
We're going on a visit
And it will be such fun.

Through the gate we know so well
And right up to the door—
We hope our teacher will be there
The way she was before.

If she's not there to say hello
Whatever shall we do?
But there's her little motor car
Still painted its bright blue.

And there's our old rope ladder
Hanging from its tree
And there are the monkey bars and tires
Just where they used to be.

"Good Morning, Mrs. Bosich,"
We say as we troop in.
"It's lovely to be back again.
Now where shall we begin?"

The Dump

Bumpety, bumpety, bump—
We're on our way to the dump.
We borrowed Dad's trailer and filled it up
With rubbish and clippings and cartons and junk.
Bumpetty, bumpety, bump—
Off we go to the dump.

The Park

We often go
To a special place
With trees and swings
And lots of space
And wildflower walks
To jog along
And little ponds
To sail boats on
And cycling paths
To ride around
And grassy banks
For rolling down
And barbeques
And picnic places
And soft green grass
For running races.
Grandpa says
It's the city's heart
This special place
We call the park.

73

OURSELVES: *Our Senses*

Looking At Me

Tall or short
Or in between?
Eyes of blue
Or brown or green?
I look in the mirror
Who do I see?
Someone I know—
Yes, it's ME!

Freckles or dimples?
Smiles or frowns?
Straight hair or curly
Yellow or brown?
I look in the mirror
Who do I see?
Someone I know—
Yes, it's ME!

Boots or sandals?
Sweaters or skirts?
Toques or beach hats?
Blouses or shirts?
I look in the mirror
Who do I see?
Someone I know—
Yes, it's ME!

Listening Ears

Take your ears
On a listening walk.
Listen to sounds
And silence and talk.
At your house
Or in the park
Down the street
And after dark
Always wear
Your listening ears.
Learn to listen
To what you hear.

Smells

Onions, toothpaste,
Petals, popcorn,
Coffee, mint,
Orange peel, toast,
Bacon, chocolate,
Lemon, cocoa—
Which one does
Your nose like most?

Feels

Here is a feel-box
Let's feel around.
Keep it a secret—
Don't tell what
You found.
Soft or hard
Round or square
There are lots of feels
To feel, aren't there?
Woolly or furry
Smooth or rough
Prickly or slippery
What else can I touch?
Put in your hand
And feel around.
Keep it a secret—
Don't tell what you found.

Tastes

A Breakfast-Time Rhyme

Boiled eggs
Fried eggs
Scrambled
Poached

Sausages
Bacon
Cheese on
Toast

Cereal
Yogurt
Orange juice
Jam

Marmalade
Cocoa
Honey
Ham

Breakfast's ready!

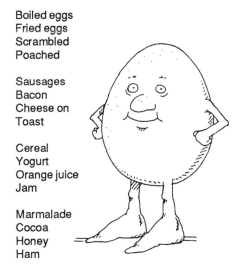

A Lunch-Time Rhyme

Peanut butter sandwich
Egg or tomato
Cheese or tuna
Chicken or ham—
Eat some healthy
Food at lunchtime.
Please don't eat
Just bread and jam.

Carrots, tomatoes,
Celery, lettuce,
Olives, sprouts,
Green onions—
Eat some healthy
Food at lunchtime.
Vegetables can
Be such fun.

Apples, pears,
Bananas, peaches,
Plums and grapes,
And apricots too—
Eat some healthy
Food at lunchtime.
You'll grow up
A stronger YOU!

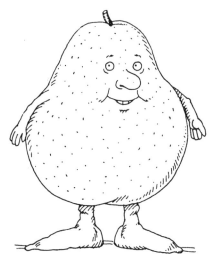

A Dinner-Time Rhyme

Pea soup
Tomato soup
Any soup
Will do

Roast lamb
Sliced ham
Casseroles
Too

Curry and rice
Are rather nice
And so is
Rich brown stew

Chops and steak
And sausages
On the
Barbecue

Green peas
Lima beans
Potatoes in
Their skins

Fresh fish
Crisp chips
Nothing out
Of tins

Fruit salad
Ice cream
Apple pie
And cheese

Tomato juice
Orange juice
No fizzy drinks
Please

Delicious food
Nutritious food
Food that's good
For you

Let's sit down
And plan a meal
A dinner just
For two.

OURSELVES: *Our Feelings*

Anger

When anger is
Inside me
I stamp and
Scream and moan.
Don't talk to me
Or touch me
I'd rather be
Alone.

When I'm feeling
Angry
I'm just not
Nice to know.
I must try to
Get over it,
I mustn't
Let it show.

So I'll do
Anything I can.
I'll close my eyes
And count to ten
And tell my anger,
"Go away!"
I won't allow it
Back again.

Happiness

How do I know
When I'm happy?

I know when I'm
Cold or hot

But I really don't know
When I'm happy

I only know
When I'm not.

Love

Every night Daddy
Sits over there
And reads his paper
In his chair
And every night
I climb on his knee
And he puts down his paper
And cuddles me.

Who's Afraid of the Bogey Man

I'm not 'fraid
Of monsters
I'm not 'fraid
Of ghosts
It's 'fraidy 'fraidy music
That makes me 'fraid
The most.

Never Talk to a Stranger

Timothy
Was in grade one
School for him
Had just begun.

"Remember, Tim,"
Said his mother,
"Don't walk home alone,
Wait for your brother."

His brother Barry
Didn't mind,
He was older than Tim
And really quite kind.

But one afternoon
Barry was late,
Timothy had to
Wait and wait.

There was no one about
Everyone had gone home
Still Tim waited
All alone.

A car pulled up
And the man inside
Sat watching Tim
For a long time.

The man got out
He said, "Hello,
Why are you standing
There alone?"

"Don't talk to strangers,"
He'd been told,
But Tim forgot.
He was tired and cold.

"Hello," he said,
"My brother's late,
He's supposed to meet me
At the gate."

"Get in my car,"
The nice man said,
"Your brother won't mind
If I take you instead."

Then a voice said,
"Yes, I do,
Come on, Tim,
I'm waiting for you."

And there was Barry
Looking stern.
The man went off
Without a word.

They watched him go,
Tim started to cry
Barry took his hand
And said, "Never mind."

"It's my fault too,
I left you alone.
I forgot the time
Come on, let's go home."

They told their mother
About the man,
And when he came home
They told their dad.

That night when the boys
Were both in bed
Their parents came in
And quietly said,

"It is hard for you
Because you are young
But you have to learn
You can't trust everyone."

"Try to remember,
Or you could be in danger,
So NEVER, NEVER
TALK TO STRANGERS."

SEASONS: *Summer*

Water

Soapy water, soapy water,
Bubbles, froth and steam,
Wash away my germs and grime
And make me fresh and clean.

Pool water, pool water,
Turquoise, green and blue,
Shining in the summer sun
Clear and deep and cool.

Stinky water, smelly water,
I find you in the pond,
I won't drink you, dirty water,
You've been there too long.

Tap water, tap water,
Boiling merrily,
Pour it in the teapot
For my cup of tea.

Rain water, rain water,
Filling up the dams,
Growing grass to feed the sheep
And their baby lambs.

Water, water, everywhere,
In lakes and seas and rivers,
In soups and stews and popsicles
And tanks and pipes and sprinklers.

We cannot do without you
You are precious, we all know,
So we must be very careful
When we use the garden hose.

Summer Memories

I have a summer memory chest
With treasures tucked inside—
This shell is like a little house
Where baby fish can hide.

We found these smooth cream pebbles
When we picnicked by the pool—
And look! A piece of coral
As pretty as a jewel.

Here's my little fishing line
In its plastic bag—
We had great fun fishing
Just Mom and me and Dad.

This is a little picture
Of our cabin by the sea—
You'll find it if you follow
Our track between the trees.

There's a bunch of daisies
I pressed inside a book—
And a candle from the birthday cake
I helped Mommy cook.

And a curvy piece of driftwood
Polished by the waves—
And a bone that looks like ivory
I found inside a cave.

And a little map of that old town
We visited last year—
And there's the old horseshoe I found
It's my favorite souvenir.

Why don't YOU make a memory chest
With treasures tucked inside?
Then, just like me, you'll always keep
Summer in your mind.

A Summer Flood

The Hopkins children lived on a farm on the prairies.

It was July, and the children were on holiday.

The wheat belt was a hot, dry, dusty place that year.

The reservoirs were usually half full.

The grass in the fields was dead and brown, and the birch trees drooped in the hot sun. Until the end of the month.

It was about nine o'clock on a Wednesday morning when it started to rain.

It rained and it rained and it rained.

The Hopkins children helped their father to shift the tractors onto higher ground, and to dig ditches around the haystacks and dumps of clover seeds.

It was still raining on Thursday morning.

Mr. Hopkins realized that things were getting very serious indeed.

He rode around the farm on his motorcycle checking the animals and the fields.

Small groups of wet, cold cattle were huddled together on every little high, dry patch of land they could find.

The reservoirs had started to overflow.

The tennis court next to the farmhouse had started to flood and it looked rather like a shallow swimming pool.

The Hopkins children helped Mr. Hopkins move the trucks and the plow out of the machinery shed and put the shivering horses in there where they could be fed and looked after.

By lunch time on Thursday everything was covered with water.

Water was everywhere.

Every creek on the property was flooded.

Water came rushing through the farmyard washing away the vegetable garden and Mrs. Hopkins' beautiful rose bushes that she loved so much.

The water flooded onto the back porch and into the house.

The Hopkins children had packed their favorite toys and books and as many clothes as they could into cartons and suitcases and Mr. Hopkins had lifted them on top of the dressers in their bedrooms.

The children helped Mrs. Hopkins store as many jars and packets and cartons of food onto the highest shelves in the kitchen and the bathroom and the laundry room.

Mrs. Hopkins' beautiful tablecloths and china were put in plastic bags, and Mr. Hopkins lifted them onto the top shelves of closets where they might escape rising water.

Some of Mrs. Hopkins' beautiful things had belonged to her mother and her grandmother. They were her treasures and she wanted to save them for her children.

The Hopkins family listened to the radio to hear what had happened to other farms in the district.

The news was very bad indeed.

Many animals had been drowned, fences had been washed away, houses flooded and bridges broken up as dams and rivers and creeks overflowed.

Mr. Hopkins went out again and again trying to help his animals.

Poor hungry cattle were trying to stay on any high ground they could find.

Mr. Hopkins could only reach the animals nearest the farmhouse with feed. The others would have to wait until the rain stopped.

All Thursday night it rained, but on Friday morning it suddenly stopped raining.

Now the really hard work had to start.

As the farm dried out, animals who had been pushed against fences or caught in the branches of trees had to be helped to safety and cared for.

Fences had to be rebuilt.

Vegetable gardens and fruit trees had to be replanted.

The dirty water and mud in the farmhouse had to be mopped and cleaned.

Mrs. Hopkins and the children had to clean walls and floors and cupboards.

Everything had to be washed—furniture, sheets, towels, curtains, blankets, clothes.

How hard everyone had to work!

The Hopkins children had often heard the stories their grandparents told about dreadful floods in the old days.

Now they had seen for themselves what the flood had done to the place they loved best in the world.

It was something they would never forget.

Summer Sounds

Clink clink
Ice in a drink

Yawning yawning
Summer morning

Crunch crunch
Salad lunch

Whirr whirr
Fans stir

Plop plip
Taps drip

Whine whine
Mosquito time

SEASONS: *Autumn*

An Autumn Diary

MONDAY: THE FIRST DAY OF AUTUMN

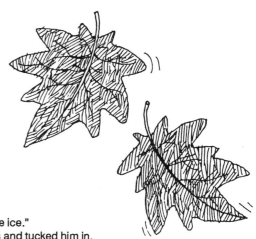

Sebastian woke up.
Something was wrong.
What was the matter with him?
He felt COLD.
At that moment he heard Natalie start to cry.
Natalie was his new baby sister.
Perhaps she was cold, too.
He heard Mommy get up and go to her.
Sebastian called to his mother.
When she came in, he told her he was COLD.
"So you are," said Mommy, cuddling him. "Your little feet are like ice."
She went to the linen cupboard and found some fleecy blankets and tucked him in.
Then she rubbed him gently until he was nice and warm, and he went back to sleep.
When it was morning Sebastian got up.
He felt VERY COLD.
Mommy came in.
"You'll need your winter sweater and pants and socks," she said.
She fetched the plastic bags from the top shelf of Sebastian's closet.
But when he put them on they were too small.
"You can't wear these," said his mother. "I should have taken you shopping last week."
"Can I wear my track suit?" asked Sebastian. "That's warm."
"Just for today, then," said Mommy, "I'll take you shopping after school."
After breakfast Sebastian's little friend, Paul, called for him.
He had his track suit on too!
As they walked to school, the warm breath from their mouths floated out on the damp cold air.
"It looks just like Grandpa's pipe smoke," said Sebastian.
That afternoon Mommy took him shopping, and Paul's mommy took Paul shopping too.
Mommy bought Sebastian new shirts, pants, a jacket, a sweater, shoes, boots, a scarf and socks, a yellow raincoat
    and hat AND two pairs of warm pyjamas AND a warm bathrobe AND slippers!
Sebastian was ready for autumn!

TUESDAY: THE SECOND DAY OF AUTUMN

It was still COLD.
Sebastian wondered if summer had gone forever.
He dressed in his new warm clothes.
Mommy cooked porridge for breakfast, and Sebastian had a mug of hot chocolate as well as his orange juice.
"Autumn weather makes us hungry," said his father.
As Sebastian and Paul set off for school they walked across Mr. Bailey's lawn.
Their feet in their new shoes left footprints on the dewy grass.
They had great fun walking round and round and in and out, making patterns all over Mr. Bailey's lawn.
Mr. Bailey came out of his front door to go to work.
When he saw what they had done he laughed.
"I used to do that when I was your age," he said.
That afternoon Sebastian's teacher, Mr. Clifton, took his class for an autumn walk.
They looked at the changes in the school garden.

Mr. Clifton explained about trees that were deciduous and trees that were evergreens, and he told the children the names of the trees.

The children made bark rubbings and collected fallen autumn leaves.

Mr. Duncan, the school gardener, told them the jobs he did in the garden in autumn.

He showed them how he planted tulip and daffodil bulbs, and how he prepared the soil for the new rose garden.

He showed them how he'd pulled out the dead summer plants and raked the autumn leaves, and mixed them together with his compost heap.

When the children went inside, Mr. Clifton told them, "We are going to make a mural about autumn at our school, and we'll make the garden part of our mural first."

The children used their bark rubbings and leaves to make a garden collage.

Autumn had come to Sebastian's classroom.

WEDNESDAY: THE THIRD DAY OF AUTUMN

"I have to take six things to school this morning," said Sebastian.

> one carrot
> one parsnip
> one turnip
> one onion
> one vegetable peeler
> one mug

"We are going to make vegetable soup."

"What a lovely idea," said his mother.

"Some parents are coming to help us, but I told Mr. Clifton about my sister Natalie's nap and he asked if you would be able to help later on."

"Of course I will," said his mother.

Everyone enjoyed making the soup.

Mr. Clifton had made a big Grade Two Recipe Book.

He printed the recipe for vegetable soup on the first page, and everyone drew vegetables around the page to make a border.

While they waited for the soup to cook, the children worked on their autumn mural.

The garden collage was nearly finished.

"We'll do the playground part next," said Mr. Clifton. "I want you to look at the clothes children are wearing and the games they are playing now that it is autumn."

By this time the soup was ready.

Everyone had a mug of soup with his lunch.

It was delicious.

Soup was just right for cold autumn days.

THURSDAY: THE FOURTH DAY OF AUTUMN

On Thursday, Sebastian had to take some old clothes to school.

"Our class is working in the vegetable garden," he told his parents."

After Mr. Duncan, the school gardener, had helped them dig up the carrots, potatoes, and turnips, they brought in the pumpkins, too.

That afternoon Mr. Clifton told them a story about how vegetables grow.

After school, Sebastian went around to his little friend Paul's house.

Paul was in bed.

He had bronchitis.

He had taken his sweater off after running around at playtime and had forgotten to put it back on, and had caught a nasty cold which had turned into bronchitis.

It is easy to catch colds in autumn.

FRIDAY: THE FIFTH DAY OF AUTUMN

Sebastian had to take his gym clothes to school, because on Friday his class has phys. ed.
"Take your raincoat," said his mother. "It looks like rain."
"But it's been fine all week," said Sebastian.
Sure enough, it started to rain at lunch time.
It rained and rained.
"I'm sorry, children," said Mr. Clifton. "I know you are disappointed. Autumn weather is very changeable."
That afternoon the children did some more work on their autumn mural.
They started on the playground section.
Everyone drew a large outline of himself on a big piece of paper and cut it out.
Then they used wool and thread and scraps of material and plastic and buttons and cord and string and ribbon
    and "filled themselves in."
Some children had drawn themselves playing football or marbles or tag or tetherball or hopscotch.
Others had drawn themselves arriving at school in their yellow raincoats.
Others were on duty-roster, cleaning dusters, picking up litter and sweeping porches, and others were dressed in
    their old clothes, working in the vegetable garden.
When they had finished, Mr. Clifton stapled the cut-out figures onto the mural.
Then the children decided to make cotton wool clouds colored white and grey and black.
They glued these onto the mural, and then they painted little patches of blue sky between the clouds.
Last of all, they made little puddles out of aluminum foil and plastic and glued them on too.
"It really looks like an autumn day," said Mr. Clifton.

SATURDAY: THE SIXTH DAY OF AUTUMN

Saturday turned out to be a fine, cold day with not a cloud in the sky.
"What a funny time of the year autumn is," thought Sebastian.
Saturday was a special day for Sebastian.
On Saturday afternoons he and his father went to the football game.
Often his grandfather came too, and on nice, sunny afternoons his mother came as well.
They took sandwiches and thermoses of hot tea and cocoa.
Sebastian and his father followed their local football team.
Sebastian had photographs of his favorite players pinned up in his bedroom.
He even had the autograph of one of them.
On Saturday nights Sebastian and his parents watched the football replays on television, and Sebastian always
    looked for pictures of his team in the Sunday papers.
He cut them out and stuck them in his scrapbook.
Sebastian and Paul often played football in Sebastian's backyard.
They practiced kicking and throwing.
Quite often Sebastian's father would play.
Autumn meant FOOTBALL to Sebastian.

SUNDAY: THE SEVENTH DAY OF AUTUMN

On Sunday morning Sebastian helped his father put the ladder, the axe, a broom, two rakes, and a shovel into the trailer.

Then off they drove to Mrs. Merriweather's house.

Mrs. Merriweather lived in the same street as Sebastian.

He had known her all his life.

She often used to baby-sit when his parents went out.

She had lots of trees and shrubs in her garden.

It was a big garden and Mrs. Merriweather was getting rather old to do heavy gardening jobs, so quite often Sebastian and his father went to her house and cleaned up her garden for her.

Sebastian's father climbed up his ladder onto the roof and swept the eavestroughs clean.

Sebastian raked the leaves on the lawn and put them into the trailer.

Mrs. Merriweather always made a special brunch for Sebastian and his father.

She knew Sebastian loved egg sandwiches and chocolate cake, so she always made them for him.

After brunch they finished loading the trailer.

Then Sebastian helped his father tie the garbage down securely.

They collected their tools and Mrs. Merriweather thanked them and gave Sebastian a little surprise she had bought for him.

It was a football jersey in blue and black, the colors of his favorite team!

Sebastian WAS pleased.

They waved goodbye and off they went to the dump.

Sebastian loved going to the dump.

He loved watching the bulldozer pushing its way through mountains of garbage and he often waved to the bulldozer driver.

He loved watching how people cleverly backed their trucks and cars and trailers into tiny little spaces.

But best of all he loved helping his father throw the garbage out.

On this Sunday morning there were more people at the dump than Sebastian had ever seen.

"I wonder why?" thought Sebastian.

"Perhaps it's got something to do with autumn."

Goodbye Summer

Carpets of autumn leaves
Softly lie
As green leaves turn yellow
And fall and die
Goodbye summer,
Goodbye, goodbye.

Cosy beds
Are tucked up tight
With woolly blankets
For cold winter nights.
Goodbye summer,
Goodbye, goodbye.

Thin little spirals
Of smoke travel high
From tall brick chimneys
And garden fires.
Goodbye summer,
Goodbye, goodbye.

Hot soups and stews
And casseroles to try.
Raincoats and sweaters
And new boots to buy.
Goodbye summer,
Goodbye, goodbye.

On the cold beach
A seagull cries
And the lonely sea breeze
Gently sighs.
Goodbye summer,
Goodbye, goodbye.

SEASONS: *Winter*

Rain

Pitter patter
Pitter patter
Rain is coming
Skitter scatter

Soup and Stew

Stir the soup
Stir the stew
A bowl for me
A plate for you

Basketball

Bounce, bounce,
Dribble, dribble,
Pass, aim, shoot—
SCORE!

It's Winter

Cough, cough,
Sneeze, sneeze,
May I have
A kleenex please?

Wet hair,
Damp clothes,
Frozen fingers,
Noses, toes.

Down-filled jackets
Bob about.
Felt-lined boots
Squelch in and out.

Mumps, bronchitis,
Sore throats, 'flu.
We're so cold
We've all turned blue.

IT'S WINTER!

Winter is Here

Branches wear diamonds
When trees lose their leaves
And summer's bright flowers
Become winter's weeds

When the pale sun is hiding
And the sky is in tears
And the warm earth turns cold
Winter is here

Puddles

Puddles in the playground
Splashing here and there
Waiting to be jumped in
Puddles everywhere.

Football

Twenty tough football players
Running down the track
Ten miles there
And ten miles back.

Twenty tough football players
Trotting on the spot
Trotting on tiptoe
Until they drop.

Twenty tough football players
Jogging down the street
Will they win on Saturday?
We'll have to wait and see.

SEASONS: *Spring*

Spring Cleaning

A little old house
Sat in the sun
And slept and dreamt
Of everyone
Who'd lived inside
Its cracked old walls
And walked along
Its creaking floors
And played in its garden
Every day
Then closed its gate
And went away.

The little old house
Belonged to the past
But it was strong
It was built to last.
It was made of wood
And iron and stone.
It had a look
All of its own
But it often felt
So alone.
If only it could
Be somebody's home.

Then one fine sunny
New spring day
It woke to hear
A soft voice say,
"What a dear little house
It's the nicest we've seen
All it needs
Is a good spring clean."
And before very long
A family moved in
With their buckets and brushes
And brooms and bins.

They washed the walls
And scrubbed the floors
And dusted the cupboards
And lined every drawer.
They cleaned the grate
And the chimney flue
And polished the brass
And the floorboards too
And everything shone
And sparkled and gleamed
And every room was
Fresh and clean.

They mended the roof
And the picket fence too
And painted it white
It looked like new.
They weeded the garden
And cleaned out the eaves
And pruned the roses
And raked the leaves.
They cut the hedge
And mowed the lawn
And trimmed the vine
Over the door.

And then at last
The spring cleaning was done
And the little old house
Smiled in the sun.
It was good to feel
So clean and bright
To breathe the fresh air
To let in the light.
The little old house
Was no longer alone
It felt cared for and loved
It felt like a home.

A Spring Diary

MONDAY

Elizabeth woke up. Something was different. Her bedroom was so light and bright. The sun was shining through her window and the sky was a pale yellow color, not dull and grey as it had been for weeks and weeks. Elizabeth's mother told her it was the first day of spring. Elizabeth wanted to wear her summer clothes to school, but her mother said although it was spring, the weather was still quite cold. Perhaps it would be warmer tomorrow. At breakfast, Elizabeth's father was coughing and sneezing. He had hay fever. He always had hay fever in the spring.

TUESDAY

Elizabeth had to take something for morning news, something about spring. What could she take? Her father had a good idea. Every year he bought Christmas cards and calendars painted by artists who used their mouths and feet to paint with because they were handicapped people who could not use their hands. Elizabeth's father showed her the calendar he had bought. For the month of April the artist had painted pretty spring wildflowers on the page. So Elizabeth took the calendar to school and talked about it at morning news time. As she walked home that afternoon Elizabeth thought about the wildflowers. There weren't any growing in her street. She wondered if there ever had been.

WEDNESDAY

On Wednesday Elizabeth's class started working on their spring theme. Some of the children were painting a spring mural and others were making spring mobiles. Miss Turner gave them some special spring homework too. They had to find three signs of spring in their neighborhood. Elizabeth thought that was easy. Daddy had hay fever, Mommy was spring cleaning, and the weather was warming up. She noticed other spring signs too. The apple tree in the garden was covered with pink and white blossoms, and the grass on the street boulevards was growing really high and thick, and Mrs. Foley, their nice old next-door-neighbor, had a new gardening hat, a pretty pink one with daisies on it. Spring had come to Elizabeth's street.

THURSDAY

It was much warmer on Thursday and Elizabeth wore her summer clothes to school. She wore a sweater too. Miss Turner had planned a surprise for her children. Because it was such a beautiful spring day, Miss Turner's class had their lunch out in the sunshine under a big tree. While they ate their lunch Miss Turner read them a spring story about a farm where lots of baby lambs were being born. It was really hot by afternoon recess so Elizabeth took off her sweater. It was lovely to feel the hot sun on her bare arms. By going-home time the sun had disappeared behind a cloud and it was quite cold. Spring really was an up and down time of the year, thought Elizabeth.

FRIDAY

Now that spring had come, the children at Elizabeth's school were starting to play different games in the playground. There were not so many puddles about and everyone brought their skipping ropes to school. The hockey season was over and the older children would soon be playing baseball. Everyone at school would be practicing for the field day. They didn't run races or anything hard like that, they played games instead, and then they had a picnic under the trees in the lovely spring weather.

SATURDAY

On Saturday while her father was golfing, Elizabeth and her mother went to visit her grandparents. Elizabeth took some asparagus from her mother's garden. Grandmother made asparagus rolls and a pot of tea. Elizabeth helped her. In winter they always sat in the sunroom where Grandmother kept her house plants, but today they sat out on the patio in the warm spring sunshine. Grandfather gave Elizabeth's mother a basket of spring flowers from his garden—daffodils, tulips, and forget-me-nots. The daisies and peonies would need some more spring sunshine before they were ready.

SUNDAY

Elizabeth had been looking forward to Sunday all week. The family was going on a picnic. Sunday was a perfect spring day, and off they went to the park to see the wildflowers and have a picnic lunch. On the way home they called into Uncle Robert's little farm in the hills. He was an artist and he spent most of his time painting in his studio. Elizabeth loved going to Uncle Robert's place especially in springtime because that was when most of the animals and birds had babies. What a lovely week it had been, thought Elizabeth, spring is the best time of the year. She wished it would last forever.

Buds

Each little bud in the garden
Has a secret wrapped inside,
Each little bud grows slowly,
Each little bud takes its time.
Each little bud sips the showers
And soaks in the warm sunshine,
And unfolds itself as a flower,
Unwrapping the secret inside.
It's a sign that winter is over
When you look in the garden and find
That each little bud is a flower
And you'll know that spring has arrived

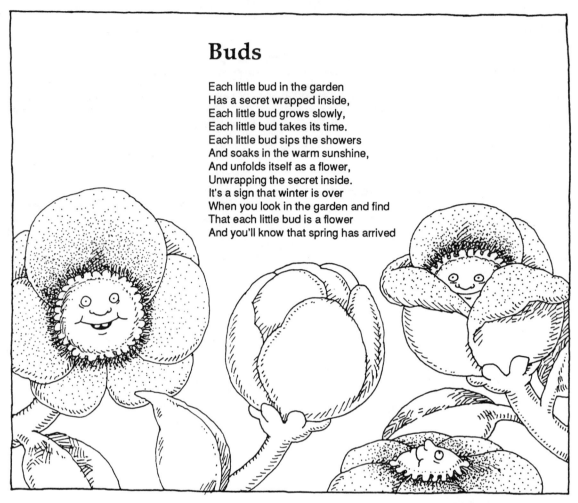

Ants

Ants, ants,
Everywhere,
Rushing here,
Rushing there.
Carrying treasures
To their nest,
Never stopping
For a rest.
Ants, ants,
Here and there,
Hurrying and scurrying
Everywhere.

Bee

One spring day
I met a bee,
Fuzzy, wuzzy
Buzzy bee,

I wish he'd stop
And talk to me,
Fuzzy, wuzzy
Buzzy bee.

But off he flew
To his hive in a tree,
Fuzzy, wuzzy
Buzzy bee.

He's so busy
Making honey,
Fuzzy, wuzzy
Buzzy bee.

Butterfly

A patch of color
In the sky.

A flutter of wings
Soft as a sigh.

A gentle visitor
Passing by.

A sign of spring,
A butterfly.

The Little Tree

"Where are my leaves?"
Cried a poor little tree,
When he woke
On a winter's day.

"I've nothing on,"
Cried the poor little tree,
"My leaves have
Blown away."

He brushed his branches
Along the ground,
But not a leaf
Could be found.

He swept his branches
Across the sky,
But not a leaf
Went flying by.

"What shall I do?"
He cried in dismay,
And he hid his face,
And turned away.

A kind old tree
In the garden next door
Whispered a secret
Over the wall.

The little tree listened
And smiled and said,
"That's what I'll do—
I'll go to bed!"

So he tucked in his branches
And closed his eyes
And went to sleep
Until spring came by.

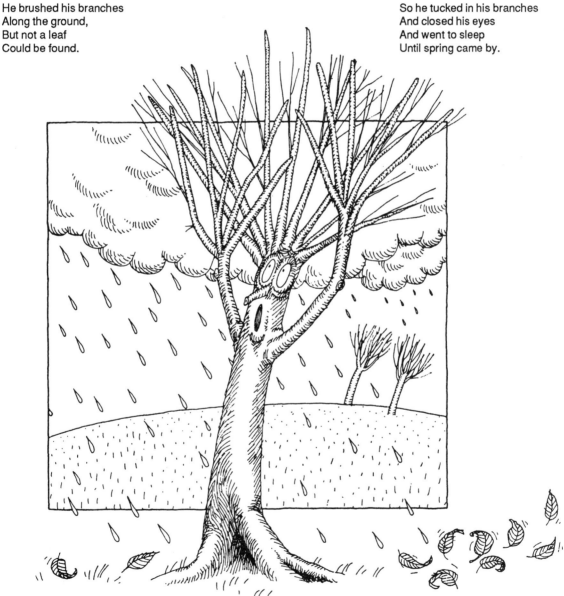

ANIMALS

Country Animals

Gyp

Gyp is a sheepdog.
He lives on a farm
He rounds up the sheep
And keeps them from harm.
He knows the farm
From end to end
The farmer calls him
His best friend.

Rabbit

A little brown rabbit
Went for a hop
He saw a carrot
And decided to stop
Munchety-munch
Crunchety-crunch
That juicy carrot
Became his lunch.

Fox

Fluffy tail
Cunning eyes
Pricked-up ears
Very wise
He comes to visit
Twice a week
When Farmer Brown
Is fast asleep.

Cows

Silly cows, stupid cows
Munching in the clover
They're so slow
They wouldn't move
If the tractor
Ran them over.

Percy Pig

Little Percy Pig
Has little pink eyes
He lives with
The other pigs
In the pig sty.

Little Percy Pig
Has a little curly tail
He eats the slops
In the farmer's pail.

Little Percy Pig
Has a little piggy voice
He says "Oink oink
Oink oink oink."

The Bull

Keep out
Take care
Prize bull
Beware!

Circus Animals

Have you ever wondered
How circus animals feel
Locked up there forever
In a house on wheels?

Have you ever wondered
What they think about
When they're made to jump through hoops
And dance and prance and bow?

Have you ever wondered
If they get tired of stares
Of people, every day and night
Always standing there?

Have you ever wondered
If they would like to be
Hunting, roaming, happy
Always running free?

Have you ever wondered
How we would behave
If we were circus animals
And lived inside a cage?

The Mouse House

In a very old street
In a very old house
Lived aristocratic
Archibald Mouse.

Archibald Mouse
And his wife, Emily,
Belonged to a very old
Mouse family tree.

The house where they lived
Of stained glass and stone,
Oak and iron lace,
Was the mouse family home.

Generations of mice
For years had lived there
In the old-fashioned pantry
Under the stairs.

So quiet were the mice
In their home down the hall
That nobody knew
They lived there at all.

The house proudly stood
In its grounds, neatly kept
But it was, on that street,
The only one left.

One day at the house
An odd stranger called.
Archibald listened
From a hole in the wall.

"I want your house,"
The odd stranger said.
"I'm going to build
An office here instead."

Archibald Mouse
Heard a soft cry
And there was Emily
By his side.

He took her paw
And held it tightly.
They listened together
Very quietly.

The owner said firmly
"Be on your way.
This family home
Is here to stay."

"This fine old house
Has been our home—
A place where past
Generations have grown."

"The city council and I
Have made a decision,
My fine old house
Will be a museum."

"Did you hear that, dear?"
Said Archibald Mouse.
"The clever owner
Has saved our house."

"Generations of mice
Will live here for years
In the old-fashioned pantry
With nothing to fear."

In a very old street
In a very old house
Lived very contented
Archibald Mouse.

Noah's Ark

CHARACTERS:

Noah, Dove, 2 Birds
Jungle Animals:

Australian Animals:
Forest Animals:

Farm Animals:
Arctic Animals:

2 monkeys, 2 lions, 2 elephants,
2 snakes, 2 tigers, 2 leopards
2 koalas, 2 emus, 2 kangaroos
2 foxes, 2 bears, 2 squirrels,
2 raccoons, 2 porcupines,
2 rabbits, 2 beavers
2 horses, 2 cows, 2 pigs, 2 goats
2 seals, 2 caribou, 2 polar
2 bears, 2 wolves, 2 walruses

NOAH:

I have been told
A great flood will come
And spread over the earth
and drown everyone.

I have built this house.
It is called an ark.
It will float on the waters
And keep us from harm.

(Calls birds to him.)

Come, little birds,
Listen to me,
Tell all the animals
You may see
That two of each kind
May live with me
Safe in my ark
'Til no floods there be.

BIRDS:
We will fly, good Noah
Over each land
And ask two of each kind
To join our band.

(Birds fly to the jungle.)

BIRDS:
We have flown to the jungle
A cruel, wild land.
Come, jungle animals,
Join our band.

MONKEYS,
LIONS, AND
ELEPHANTS:
The monkeys, the lions,
The elephants too,
Cried, "Thank you, birds.
We'll come with you."

TIGERS AND
LEOPARDS:
Tigers and leopards
To name just a few
Decided to come
And many more, too.

(Birds fly to Australia.)

BIRDS:
We have flown to Australia
A quiet, gentle, land.
Come, Australian animals
Join our band.

KOALAS,
EMUS, AND
KANGAROOS:
The emus, the koalas
And kangaroos, too
Cried, "Thank you, birds.
We'll come with you."

(Birds fly to the forest.)

BIRDS:
We have flown to the forest
A green, soft land.
Come, forest animals
Join our band.

FOXES,
BEARS, AND
SQUIRRELS:
The foxes, the squirrels
The growly bears too
Cried, "Thank you, birds.
We'll come with you."

RACCOONS AND
PORCUPINES:
Raccoons and porcupines
Came down to the shore
They boarded the ark
And then there were more.

RABBITS AND
BEAVERS:
Rabbits and beavers
To name just a few
Decided to come
And many more too.

(Birds fly to the farm.)

BIRDS:
We have flown to the farm
A kind, busy land.
Come, farm animals
Join our band.

HORSES, COWS, AND PIGS:	The horses and cows And the grimy pigs too Cried, "Thank you, birds. We'll come with you."
SHEEP AND GOATS:	The sheep and the goats To name just a few Decided to come And many more too.

(Birds fly to the Arctic.)

BIRDS:	We have flown to the Arctic, A freezing, white land. Come, Arctic animals, Join our band.
CARIBOU, SEALS, AND POLAR BEARS:	The caribou and the seals And the polar bears too Cried, "Thank you, birds. We'll come with you."
WOLVES AND WALRUSES:	The wolves and the walruses To name just a few Decided to come And many more too.

(Birds fly back to Noah.)

BIRDS:	We have flown, good Noah Over each land. We've found two of each kind To join our band.
NOAH:	Thank you, birds A job well done Now line up please I must count everyone.

(Animals line up and march into Ark.)

NOAH:	Two pigs and two cows And many more too So many to save So much to do.

Two goats, two lions
Two snakes and two bears
Two foxes, two squirrels
Two horses are there.

Two emus, two koalas
And two kangaroos
Two seals, two caribou
And two polar bears too.

At last they're all safe
And here comes the rain.
We'll lift off the ground
And then sail away.

(Animals sway.)

ANIMALS:	And then the rain rained And then the wind blew For forty long nights And forty days too.
NOAH:	*(Rubs eyes.)* I'm sure I'm not dreaming. It seems to me At last it's stopped raining. Can this really be? *(Beckons dove.)* Come, gentle dove I'll set you free To search for news And return to me. *(Dove flies off, returns with twig.)*
DOVE:	This twig, good Noah From a green olive tree Means the rain has gone Do come and see.
NOAH:	I'll open the door And look about— Why, the rain has gone. The sun has come out! Come now animals It's time to go The flood has gone. You can find your way home.
ANIMALS:	Thank you, good Noah For being so kind And giving us shelter And saving our lives. We are sad to leave Our home in the ark. It has made us safe And kept us from harm. *(Animals march off in pairs,* *waving to Noah.)*
NOAH:	My strong, sturdy ark— A job well done. You have saved the animals— Every one. *(Noah waves goodbye to the animals.)* And now it's all over We are tired, you and I. Let's rest in the sunshine And sleep for a while.

HOLIDAYS

Going on a Picnic

Our holidays
Have just begun
Holidays are
Lots of fun
We're going on
A picnic today
To a favorite spot
Our car knows the way!

They're lots of chores
For us to do
Dad packs the drinks
And the barbecue
Mom packs the meat
And salad and fruit
Gran packs the plates
And cutlery too.

We pack the bats
And the baseballs
We know what to do
We've done it before
We pack the rugs
And Gran's folding chair
At last we're off
We'll soon be there.

Going Skating

Left foot, right foot
Left foot, right
We're learning to skate
So hold on tight.

Right foot, left foot
Right foot, left
Whoops! Crash!
Get up again!

Leave the rail
Just let it go
Skate around slowly
On your own.

Turns and circles
Figures of eight
Now you really
Can roller-skate!

Going to the Movies

"It's raining," cried Tim
As he jumped out of bed.
"We can't go fishing,"
Christopher said.
"Dad, may we go to a movie instead?"

Dad looked at Mother.
They heard her say,
"I suppose it's one way to
spend a wet day."

They looked in the paper
To see where to go.
Then off they went
To the movie show.

Going Canoeing

Dip your paddle in and out
Along the river we glide
Just we two in our canoe
Exploring as we ride.

A Camping Holiday

Jamie McDonald was excited. His friend, Raoul Santos was coming to stay at his house for the first weekend of the July holidays. Jamie's big brother Lou was going camping with the scout troop.

"Raoul's going to sleep in your bed, Lou," said Jamie.

"Only if Lou doesn't mind," said Mother.

"I don't mind, Mom," said Lou. "Little brother might get frightened sleeping in a room by himself."

Jamie hated being teased. He wished his parents were rich so he and Lou could have their own bedrooms and not have to share.

Dad took pity on Jamie. "If Lou is going camping I don't see why Jamie shouldn't too," he said. "If Raoul's parents agree, the two of you could camp out in the back garden on Saturday night."

And so it was arranged. Jamie and Raoul spent hours planning. They made out a list of things to take—sleeping bags, a compass, a whistle, flashlights, games. All Saturday afternoon they helped Jamie's father set up his old tent in the garden. Then they carried in their provisions.

Mrs. McDonald had packed some food for the boys in case they got hungry in the night—peanut butter sandwiches, boiled eggs, salt and pepper, a bag of peanuts, and a bag of raisins to chew. Mrs. Santos gave Raoul some big green juicy apples and a chocolate cake as well.

The boys helped Jamie's mother make some cocoa in thermoses, in case they got thirsty.

After tea on Saturday night the boys said "Goodnight" to Jamie's parents. Mrs. McDonald said she would leave the back light on but the boys said "No thank you, we can manage." So out in the dark they went, shining their flashlights along the garden path, past the tool shed, through the gate in the hedge to the back of the garden where it was really dark and quiet.

They secured the tent flap and checked their provisions. Jamie noticed that Raoul had brought two plastic bags with him.

"What's in there?" asked Jamie.

"Hand grenades," said Raoul.

"Hand grenades?" exclaimed Jamie. "What do you want them for?"

"In case a boa constrictor crawls into the tent in the night," said Raoul.

"What's a boa constrictor?" asked Jamie, really alarmed, but trying not to show it.

"It's in that poem Mrs. Mandy read to us in class," said Raoul. "You know Jamie—I'm being swallowed by a boa constrictor, it's up to my knees, my neck—that one. Anyway they're not really grenades. They're soggy lemons Mom was going to throw out."

Jamie knew Raoul always did well in creative writing and drama at school. He was imaginative, so when he announced, "I'm no longer Raoul Santos. I'm John Frederick Seaview," Jamie wasn't surprised at all. He just said, "Who?"

"I'm John Frederick Seaview, the first pioneer to settle in this district. Your street is named after me—"Seaview Terrace." This spot will be where I'll build my house."

Jamie's street *was* called Seaview Terrace. Not to be outdone he said, "And I'm no longer Jamie McDonald either, I'm captain Neil Armstrong and this tent is my spaceship. This is not a garden, this is a moonscape."

But Raoul wasn't listening. He was pulling what looked like a bundle of sticks and string out of the other plastic bag. "I nearly forgot to set up the trap," he said. He went to the opening of the tent and started pushing the sticks into the ground and then he tied the string across and round the sticks to make a neat trap. "Just in case a dinosaur or a sabre-toothed tiger decides to visit us in the night," he said.

Jamie checked his alarm clock and set it for half past six.

"Let's have something to eat," he said. So they had some cocoa and sandwiches and played a game of snakes and ladders. Then they wriggled into their sleeping bags and turned off their flashlights. It was very dark in the little tent, and it was very quiet outside—no night sounds at all, just silence. The boys felt warm and safe and very pleased with themselves as they went quietly fast asleep.

They hadn't been asleep very long when they were woken by a roaring, grunting, growling noise. They were so frightened they nearly jumped out of their sleeping bags.

"What is it?" cried Jamie, trying to find his flashlight.

"Whatever it is, I'm going to stop it" yelled Raoul. Even in the dark his hand found his lemons and he started to pitch them with all his strength in the direction of the noise.

"Cut that out," roared a voice Jamie knew. At the same moment Jamie found his flashlight…there was his father lying on the ground tangled up in string and sticks and blankets and dripping with soggy lemons.

The two boys stared in horror.

"It was getting cold," said Jamie's father, "and Mom thought you might need some blankets."

Then Mother arrived. She'd heard the racket from the house. When she saw Jamie's father she started to laugh. Then Jamie's father laughed. And Jamie laughed. And then even Raoul laughed. They untangled Mr. McDonald and helped to wipe him down, and Jamie and Raoul picked up the soggy lemons and put them back in the plastic bag.

Then the four of them sat down in the little tent and had a drink of cocoa. Then Jamie's father and mother went back to the house.

I can hardly wait to tell Lou about our camping out," said Jamie sleepily.

"I'll never forget tonight," said Raoul. "It's been such fun."

And do you know, he never did.

NEWSPAPERS

Reading the Paper

What does Grandfather
Read in the paper?
What does Grandfather
Read?
Weather, crosswords
And who won the game—
That's what Grandfather
Reads.

What does Mother
Read in the paper?
What does Mother
Read?
Specials to buy
For the family—
That's what Mother
Reads.

What does Uncle
Read in the paper?
What does Uncle
Read?
Gardening notes
About seeds and weeds—
That's what Uncle
Reads.

What does Grandmother
Read in the paper?
What does Grandmother
Read?
Births and deaths
And recipes—
That what Grandmother
Reads.

What does Auntie
Read in the paper?
What does Auntie
Read?
Fashions and diets
And films to see—
That's what Auntie
Reads.

What do the children
Read in the paper?
What do the children
Read?
Comics and riddles
Jokes and stories
That's what the children
Read.

What does Father
Read in the paper
What does father
Read?
News and Lotto
And what's on TV—
That's what Father
Reads.

That's what our family
Reads in the paper
That's what our family
Reads.
We'd like to know
So tell us please
What does your family
Read?

A Class Newspaper

We're going to start
A newspaper
Our teacher said
We could
He asked us if
We wanted to
We rather thought
We should
'Cause now that we
Are in grade three
And read and write
And spell
We've lots of things
To write about
And lots of news
To tell.

Letters to the Editor

Dear Fairy Godmother,

I have a problem. I don't like going
to bed in the dark. I know I'm too
big to be frightened but I can't help it.

Please help me solve my problem.

Baby Bear

Dear Fairy Godmother,

Why do I always have to eat things
I don't like? My mother says they
are good for me.

Can you think of any way to make
the foods I don't like taste better?

Cookie Monster

Dear Fairy Godmother,

My mother has always warned me
about talking to strangers, but
I don't know what to do when the
Wolf comes up to me and tries to
talk to me.

Please help me.

Red Riding Hood

Dear Fairy Godmother,

I'm not sure, but I think I've got
bad manners. I know the Three
Bears are cross with me because I
went into their house without being
invited and I ate up their food and
broke their things.

I don't like it when other people
don't like me.

Goldilocks

Births & Deaths

When Father reads his paper
Each morning he will find
Notices of births and deaths
Printed side by side.

In our class newspaper
These notices you'll find
Births—Peter's cat had kittens.
Deaths—Sally's budgie died.

Advertisements

Today is sale day
At our store.

Prices slashed
And bargains galore.
Discounts found
On every floor.

Are we ready?
OPEN THE DOORS!

Lost & Found

If you find
Somebody's pet
Don't read the page
Which says
"For Rent"
Turn to
"Lost and Found"
Instead!

Sporting Results

Who won the football game?
What were the scores?

Who won the volleyball game?
Was it a draw?

Who won the soccer game?
Was it two-all?

Look up the paper
Just to make sure.

Competitions

Puzzles and crosswords?
We've done those.
Jokes and riddles?
They're all right, I suppose.
But the competition we like best
Is the "Write Your Own Jingle"
Poetry quest.
So we sat down
And made up a few
Mixed-up nursery rhymes
Just for you.
Jingles of a reasonable size
And guess what?
We won first prize!
(You'll find them on page 101)

Nursery Rhymes We Made Up Ourselves

Humpty Dumpty
And Raggedy Annie
Went to the country
To visit their granny.
Milked the cows
And made the cheese
Drove the tractor
And picked some peas.
Humpty Dumpty
And Raggedy Annie
Love the country
And visiting Granny.

Jack and Jill
And Bo-Peep too
Took Miss Muffet
To the zoo.
They saw some seals
And snakes and bears
And lions and tigers
While they were there.
They had a ride
On the little zoo train
But they had to go home
'Cause it started to rain.

Wee Willie Winkie
And Little Boy Blue
Went to the shops
And Polly went too.
They pushed their carts
To and fro
Up the aisles
And down the rows.
They bought some eggs
And bread and honey
And went to the check-out
To pay the money.
They got back home
At half-past three
And Willie put the kettle on
And made a cup of tea.

Matthew, Mark,
Luke and John
Went to bed
With their nightcaps on
Like four little teapots
Tucked in bed
With four tea cosies
On their heads.